III	IV	TARGET

Test: Use examples and counterexamples to test for necessity and sufficiency.

4. Keep, modify, or reject the feature(s) on the basis of the test(s).

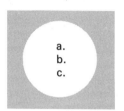

a.
b.
c.

Generic
features
of X

Search for distinguishing marks which can be used to separate types.

4. Test the typology developed with examples and counterexamples schematizing relations between types.

1   2
3

Different
types
of X

Revise the condition to meet the context problem or select an additional condition and test it (as in 2).

4. Test the necessity and sufficiency of the conditions arrived at.

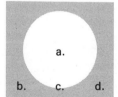

a.

b.   c.   d.

Context
conditions
for X

An Introduction to the Analysis of Educational Concepts

SECOND EDITION

Jonas F. Soltis

PROFESSOR OF PHILOSOPHY AND EDUCATION
TEACHERS COLLEGE, COLUMBIA UNIVERSITY

Addison-Wesley Publishing Company

Reading, Massachusetts
Menlo Park, California
London
Amsterdam
Don Mills, Ontario
Sydney

0380983

Second printing, April 1978

ISBN 0-201-06989-X
ABCDEFGHIJ-AL-798

For Nancy and Mystic

Preface to the second edition

Perhaps the most frequent reason for revising a text is to bring it up to date and to include in it new developments that have transpired in the field since the earlier edition. This is *not* why I have revised this text. Except for an updated bibliography, the old substantive material dealt with in the first edition of a dozen years ago has been retained, and even the addition of a new chapter, "Teaching Revisited," deals mainly with Paul Komisar's ideas from over a decade ago. This is not to say that much has not been accomplished by philosophers working at the analysis of educational concepts during the interim. In fact, quite the contrary is true, especially with the rapid development of the analytic treatment of educational ideas in Great Britian led by R. S. Peters at the University of London and the training of young philosophers of education in the United States and Canada at such institutions as Teachers College of Columbia University, Harvard, Ohio State University, the University of Illinois, Temple, Simon Fraser University, the Ontario Institute for Studies in Education, and others.

But, like all fields that develop rapidly, there comes with such development a growth in sophistication of technique and treatment of ideas which usually demands a fairly thorough acquaintance with the literature before one can understand the points being made. In revising this book, therefore, I was guided by the simple principle that beginners begin better at the beginning. So, in this version of the text, I have kept the less complex literature which I dealt with a dozen years ago, because it has proved over the years to be a good substantive vehicle for introducing people to analytic thinking about education and to some of the basic techniques of philosophical analysis. I viewed this book then, as well as now, as a primer, a simple introduction to a very effective way of thinking about education. This is the major task once again undertaken, with very little revision in the first four chapters of the book. I have added a new fifth chapter, which provides an example of a bit more complex analysis, to serve as an illustrative bridge for those who want to cross over to some of the more sophisticated contemporary literature. I have also added a new epilogue to provide instruction and practice in analytic-skills development, an area not fully considered in the first edition.

The real reason for undertaking this revision, then, was not to include new literature and ideas, but to make good use of what I and others who have used this book as a teaching device have learned over the years about helping people to learn how to think analytically. In the earlier edition I tried to point to the techniques of analysis which were being used in the text to examine certain educational concepts, so that students could see not only the results of the analysis, but also how it was done. I named such simple techniques as "asking prior questions," "using counterexamples," and "making distinctions," and over the years I have been able to add to this list. In fact, I have found with others that if you can name and describe techniques, students are better able to see and grasp them as ways of thinking and of clarifying thought.

What I have tried to do in this revision, therefore, is to enhance this emphasis on analytic techniques and strategies in two ways: first, by doing more naming and describing; and, second, by providing the opportunity for practice in analytic-skill development. In each of the first four chapters I have tried to focus more attention on the techniques and strategies employed, first by highlighting the introduction of each new technique or strategy with the use of boldface type at its first naming and then by reflectively describing the steps of each basic strategy after using it. To the above-named techniques, I also have added new descriptions of three basic analytic strategies, which I have called "generic-type analysis," "differentiation-type analysis," and "conditions-type analysis." For those familiar with the first edition, a generic-type analysis names the kind of analysis done in Chapter 2 with the concept of a "discipline" and differentiation-type analysis refers to the kind of work done there on the concept of "subject matter." My earlier analysis of the subjective dimension of explanation fits the form of a conditions-type analysis.

I have found in my own classes that students are better able to see, understand, and imitate these general strategies if the strategies are named and described. Therefore, I also have added to the second edition of this text a new epilogue which is designed to provide for the pedagogy of analytic-skills development. The epilogue in the first edition contained an annotated bibliography of relevant literature in the field. My intention there was to provide students, after their brief introduction to the techniques and substance of an analytic approach to educational concepts, with an easy entry into the basic literature now available to them. While I think that the annotated bibliography served its purpose well in the early years of the development of the philosophical analysis of educational concepts, I now feel that the shift in emphasis in this second edition toward providing more fully for the opportunity to develop analytic skills is better served by the sharing of what I and others have learned about teaching toward these ends. So, that early epilogue is gone and a new one stands in its place.

Essentially, the new epilogue provides simple examples and thumbnail descriptions of the basic techniques and strategies used in the text and also offers suggestions for reviewing them and for practicing their use. It is hoped that this new epilogue will be useful for instructors looking for ways to help students develop the skills of analysis and for students themselves who might wish to go to each section of the epilogue after each chapter to better understand and to practice the techniques and strategies just demonstrated. Learning any skill takes practice and my students over the years prodded me to invent simple and direct exercises to help them feel that they know what they are about. The exercises and suggestions included here are the result. I should like to make clear that while the techniques and strategies outlined in this book are essentially those of the philosopher, I have not used this text to try to make philosophers of students in a single semester. Nevertheless, while the majority of my students are preparing for careers in areas of education other than philosophy, almost to a person they find that developing skills for clear thinking is a very valuable outcome of a single course in analytic philosophy, an outcome that can be usefully applied to any chosen field of education. For this and many other reasons outlined above, I hope this revision carries a step further my intention of the first edition: to provide people with an introduction to both the *substance* and the *skills* of contemporary philosophical analysis of educational concepts.

While I think I owe my greatest debt to the many students who have worked through my basic course in the analysis of educational concepts, I also owe a very heavy debt to Donna Kerr and Thomas

White, who served as preceptors in that course at a very crucial time in its development. I had reached a point of thinking that the course was as effective as it could be expected to be and that there wasn't really a lot new to be done pedagogically. Both showed me how wrong I was and urged me to continue to think about how to teach people to think analytically. I am also especially indebted to Donna Kerr, who continued teaching a similar course at the University of Washington in Seattle after completing her degree at Teachers College and as a reviewer of the manuscript shared with me fully what she has learned in the process. I have used her good ideas freely in this edition. Dick Pratt and Gerry Reagan of Ohio State and a number of good and able teaching assistants in Philosophy of Education there also deserve thanks for using my first text effectively and for helping me to see many ways to improve on its use when I visited there in 1973. Dick Pratt also served as a reviewer of the manuscript, as did Nicholas Appleton of Arizona State. Both freely offered many excellent suggestions, most of which I have tried to incorporate in this edition of the text. Cathy Redlich of Addison-Wesley provided the sensitive editorial work which has made my ponderous prose more presentable. I also would like to thank Warren Goodell for typing the revised manuscript and for suggesting that I put student exercises at the end of the volume. Mary Linn Marks provided very able assistance with a portion of the bibliography. My wife, Nancy, deserves special recognition for holding so many things together and still while I struggled to put the final pieces of the effort together. Finally, I would like to thank President Lawrence Arthur Cremin of Teachers College, Columbia University, for releasing me from administrative duties so that I might return to full time scholarship and teaching. Accordingly, I also dedicate this edition to the President, Deans, and Directors of T.C. who have masterfully ministered the College while I mended my manuscript on Mondays.

New York City   J.F.S.
October 1977

Preface to the
first edition

This book grew directly out of my courses in philosophy of education, developed over recent years at Wesleyan University and Columbia Teachers College and taught to students with varied academic backgrounds and equally heterogeneous career goals in education. It is designed to introduce anyone without a background in philosophy to a new way of approaching and examining quite ordinary yet central ideas which are fundamental to the everyday business of educating.

Long before I had ever given any thought to a career in education, I was introduced to the 20th century revolution in philosophy called "philosophical" or "linguistic" analysis. I recall being quite impressed by the no-nonsense attitude of such philosophizing and by the stringent demands it made for clarity and precision in dealing with traditional philosophical ideas. But more than this, I saw then in the analytic approach a potential to build bridges between philosophy and reality, theory and practice, idea and action. Later, while studying philosophy of education at Harvard, I found that the techniques of philosophical analysis were being applied effectively by contemporary philosophers to the language and concepts of education, and so my initial attraction to analysis merged with my newfound concerns in education. "Philosophy of education" then ceased to be so remote from educational practice as it had once seemed to me, and became more immediately and directly tied to the daily tasks of the classroom teacher, the school administrator, the curriculum developer, and other practicing educators. I became convinced that the most important tools of the trade in education are those concepts that are used to think about, guide, and control the ongoing educative process, and that a clear understanding of these concepts is an essential prerequisite to dealing intelligently with any educational activity.

So I came to write this book. In its preparation I have drawn heavily from many recent works by my analytic colleagues to provide the reader with this introduction to their current and ongoing efforts in the analysis of educational concepts, and also to provide a springboard for moving beyond what has already been accomplished in this sector of philosophy of education. My debt to such philosophers will be most apparent to those who read this book, but in this preface I must single out for special recognition Professor Israel Scheffler, under whom I had the privilege to study at Harvard. I am especially in his debt for the extensive use of many basic analytic ideas which he developed in his pioneering works in this field. Although these are individually acknowledged in the text, I must frankly admit that there would be little substance to introduce the reader to were it not for his continued efforts through the years to deal analytically with many basic educational concepts and his unpretentious provision of a first-rate model of the analytic philosopher in action.

I cannot end this preface without also generally acknowledging a host of unnamed scholars and teachers who have influenced my thoughts and writing over the years, nor can I omit my debt to the Columbia Council for Research in the Humanities for their generous grant to work on the early stages of this book in the summer of 1966. For other funds made available to me by the Columbia Teachers College Faculty Research Fund, I also offer my sincere gratitude. For most able and thorough bibliographical assistance, my thanks go to Mr. Larry Smircich; and for her conscientious job of typing this manuscript, I thank Miss Janet Abernathy. Thanks, too, to Professor Robert Guttchen, who read the completed manuscript and offered many valuable suggestions, some of which I used to my advantage and some of which I disregarded at my peril. Last but not least I must also recognize the many students who have offered much in my courses and not only provided me with some excellent ideas, but also with some confirmation of my belief that philosophical analysis has much to offer the beginning and practicing educator.

New York   J.F.S.
January 6, 1968

Acknowledgments

I am grateful to the following for permission to reprint from works on which they hold copyright:

Humanities Press for selections from "Education as Initiation," by R. S. Peters, in *Philosophical Analysis and Education*, R. A. Archambault, ed. (1965) • *Phi Delta Kappan* for selections from "On Becoming an Intellectual Discipline," by Sherwin S. Shermis (1962) • Philosophical Library for selections from *An Introduction to the Philosophy of Education*, by D. J. O'Connor (1957) • Rand McNally for selections from "Uses of Subject Matter," by Kenneth B. Henderson, in *Language and Concepts in Education*, B. O. Smith and R. H. Ennis, eds. (1961) • Routledge and Kegan Paul Ltd. for selections from *An Introduction to the Philosophy of Education*, by D. J. O'Connor (1957); and from "Education as Initiation," by R. S. Peters, in *Philosophical Analysis and Education*, R. A. Archambault, ed. (1965) • Scott, Foresman for selections and paraphrased material from *The Conditions of Knowledge*, by Israel Scheffler (1965) • Studies in Philosophy and Education, Incorporated, and The Philosophy of Education Society for revised excerpts from "The Subject Dimension of Explanation," by Jonas F. Soltis in *Proceedings of the Twenty-First Annual Meeting of the Philosophy of Educa-*

tion Society, Francis T. Villemain, ed. (1965)   •   The University of Wisconsin Press and the Regents of the University of Wisconsin for selections from *The Discipline of Education,* John Walton and James L. Kuethe, eds. (1963).   •   *Theory Into Practice,* for revised excerpts from "The Passion to Teach," by Jonas F. Soltis (1973).

Contents

Introduction

This is a book about thinking about education and how to bring clarity to our thoughts. John Dewey once made a most perceptive distinction between "thinking" and "thought." Thinking, he observed, is an active, vital, dynamic process full of adventure and excitement; thought is the end of this process, both its fruit and its demise unless the thought arrived at by thinking leads to more thinking and to more effective doing. In a way, much of what has been offered in introductory courses in philosophy of education at our colleges and universities has been thought, the results produced by great thinkers who have struggled with educational problems and ideas in an attempt to present a sensible theoretical view of education. In such courses, students often are asked merely to load their baskets with the thoughts of others and store them away for future use in their lives as educators. They seldom engage in the rigor and adventure of the thinking process itself.

This, of course, is an exaggerated charge, but I am sure that it rings true for many students who have found the excitement of actively thinking about education lacking in their basic education courses. What this book is intended to demonstrate, therefore, is that an introduction to educational thought need not neglect instruction in the techniques of philosophical thinking nor slight the opportunity to engage individuals in a personal unraveling of educational concepts. Philosophical thinking, however, isn't making the world over to agree with one's own values or views about things, nor is it just the spinning out of a lot of good ideas. Philosophical thinking is careful and controlled thinking directed at clarifying how we think and what we think about. In the twentieth century, an acknowledged "revolution in philosophy" has put heavy emphasis on the important role the philosopher plays in clarifying the concepts we use to order and operate in our everyday world. This book is aimed at getting non-philosophers to see how this mode of philosophizing is done and, for those who would try, at teaching them how to do it in a rudimentary way.

Perhaps the most difficult thing to do when reading a book of this sort is to put aside temporarily the interesting ideas and pay attention to *how* those ideas were arrived at. Whether this book can be successful in communicating both substantive educational ideas and methodological techniques will depend in great part on the reader's perseverance, ability, and willingness to follow this dual approach to its conclusion, working and thinking along the way. However, all that really is essential to the reader of this book is common sense, which, as DesCartes once remarked, must be the most abundant and evenly distributed quality among men, because in all his life he never heard anyone complain that he lacked it.

The substance of this book is deceptively simple to specify; concepts like subject matter, teaching, and learning are quite ordinary and central to the educational enterprise. As such, they provide a basic point of departure for anyone concerned with education—from the layman and neophyte to the accomplished educational practitioner and scholar. Yet they quickly become puzzling ideas, which, on careful examination, lead to a chain of inquiry in which each link is frequently another provocative question rather than a conclusive answer. Those who look to a book on educational philosophy for facts, information, and final answers are likely to feel frustrated. But such a finished work, in my judgment, is a very poor instrument for helping people learn how to think philosophically. Thus, the emphasis here will not be on finding satisfying answers, but on provoking thought by examining and questioning some basic educational concepts. Moreover, the reader will be given direct instruction in certain techniques and strategies of thinking analytically used by contemporary philosophers to examine ideas in many fields.

Fortunately, neither education nor thinking is totally foreign to any of us. We've all spent a good part of our lives being educated and we devote at least some of our time to thought. Nonetheless, our knowledge of thinking and education probably has not been philo-

sophically examined or ordered. This book provides the means to do
just that.

I have said that this book has an unusual dual approach and that
readers may find it difficult to learn to read for two things at once.
While I hope that the substance of the text is interesting and useful,
I have tried also to help people reflect on the techniques and strategies of analysis being demonstrated and described in the text. Of
course, pointing to skills and techniques is not the same as teaching.
It's much like providing nonswimmers with a description and demonstration of the crawl and then throwing them into water over their
heads. The results are bound to be disastrous.

A reviewer of this manuscript* suggested an analogy that helps
to clarify the book's intent: imagine trying to teach people the skills
of carpentry without first giving them practice with the various tools
of the carpenter. Furthermore, not only is practice with hammers,
saws, planes, and levels necessary, but people must practice on something. One could, for example, learn how to use carpentry tools by
building a birdhouse, much as I try in this book to teach the tools of
analysis by examining educational ideas. Most beginners, however,
are more apt to focus on the finished product—the birdhouse, or the
substantive ideas about education—rather than on the tools and
techniques. It is a very normal thing to do. But if this book is to be
an effective introduction to the analysis of educational concepts, one
must give equal attention to both substance and methodology.

Because focus on method is not usually the point of textbooks,
readers will need to try all the harder to grasp this part of the book.
To help in this pursuit, I have provided an epilogue, which contains a
number of simple examples to aid understanding, as well as practical,
straightforward suggestions for practicing the skills and techniques
demonstrated and described in this book. These have come from
years of experience using this material with students. Some might
find it helpful to refer to the epilogue after reading each chapter;
others may use it as a convenient summary of the methodologies discussed.

In the chapters that follow, we begin by asking some general
questions about the concept of education itself, which underscore
both its complexity and its vagueness. We look closely into what
might be called "the logic of definitions of education" and into what
it means to have an educational aim. These topics introduce the analytic techniques of *asking prior questions* and *making distinctions*.
Then, we briefly consider debates concerning the academic status of

---

*   Professor Richard Pratte of Ohio State University.

this subject called "education," so that we may introduce the analytic strategy of *generic-type analysis,* a means of clarifying a concept by identifying its key characteristics. We also use this discussion of the concept of a "discipline" to demonstrate the technique of using *counterexamples*—that is, sharpening up the meaning of an idea by pointing to examples that test and refine our conceptions by negative instances.

There will be fewer answers than questions in these early pages, but all this is merely a warm-up, a first brush with analytic techniques. Only when we move on to examine the concepts of "subject matter" and "knowledge" will we begin to get to the heart of the educational enterprise. And, as we turn to an examination of "teaching," "learning," and "understanding," we shall find ourselves deeply immersed in those ideas most relevant to the classroom situation. We also use this substantive discussion to introduce the reader to the analytic strategies of *differentiation-type analyses* and *conditions-type analyses,* and to a more complex application of the multiple techniques of analysis.

Then, just as we begin to ask the right kinds of questions and to get a feel for the basic techniques and strategies used by analytic philosophers, we stop to survey the limits and uses of thinking analytically about ordinary educational ideas. To clearly set some of these limits and to demonstrate some practical applications of analysis, we first examine the nature of disagreements over educational values and then broadly consider the general function and features of the language of education itself.

With that, this introduction to the analysis of educational concepts will be complete, but our journey together will not yet be over. As noted above, the epilogue is intended to serve both as a summary of the techniques of analysis and as a set of suggestions for learning these techniques and strategies. The bibliography that follows is an invitation to the reader to continue the endless journey of thinking about and examining those educational ideas that guide educational practice.

At this point, it should be clear that I treat philosophy as an activity and not as an answer. It is careful and critical thinking about what one cares about and does. This book provides a way for educators to learn to do just that. Our course is set. We will move through a morass of complex ideas, examine their logical underpinnings, and attempt to gain appreciation of and skill with analytic techniques and strategies. Comforting and inspiring thoughts are not what we are seeking. Rigorous, clear, and precise thinking will be our standard and we will let the chips and cherished ideas fall where they may.

So as not to frighten off potential readers by what may seem to be an extremely unromantic and complicated analytic approach to philosophizing about education, let me hastily add that this work itself is not technically analytic—it is not necessary to have previously studied philosophy to be able to understand what follows. On the contrary, any fluent speaker of English should be able to manage and master at an elementary level the techniques of analytic thinking introduced, if willing to probe his or her own unexamined thoughts and the ideas of others and to practice the techniques and strategies outlined herein. This is a book written for anyone who is or intends to become an educator and who wants to learn to think more clearly about what he or she is doing. Although the book omits the thought of the great, classical educational philosophers and the basic philosophical positions of educational movements or "schools," I do not want to give the impression that they are irrelevant or meaningless. Rather, I would suggest that, once educators become genuinely excited about thinking critically and carefully about education, they may then find more value in an examination of classical and contemporary educational thought.

Ideally, an introduction should whet the appetite and provide the skills for further and more intimate contact with a field of study. It is toward this goal that this book in philosophy of education is directed. Let me now invite the reader to begin the journey by first meeting the familiar and ordinary concept of education itself.

Education and analysis

1

To examine ideas which are in such common currency in one's life that they are seldom if ever reflected on can be a most puzzling and yet gratifying intellectual venture. Ordinarily, however, very few of us do this: doctors don't stop to think about "Medicine" as an area of human endeavor in which they are totally involved, nor do lawyers unduly concern themselves with a thorough examination of the concept of "The Law." In fact, outside of the academic classroom, where a course in a specified subject area seems inevitably to begin with a definition of the field to be studied, few people attempt to clarify just what is meant by the terms denoting their own fields of endeavor. And, even though teachers are notorious for defining the boundaries and major landmarks of the fields they are about to explore with students, I would guess that most who teach or who are students seldom, if ever, reflect carefully and systematically on the ideas central to the educational tasks they are about.

Students and teachers may feel that to ask such ridiculous questions as: "What is meant by 'teaching'? 'learning'? or 'subject matter'?" is like asking a storekeeper to reflect on the meaning of "buying," "selling," or "merchandise." After all, such ordinary terms hardly seem to call for an unnecessary strain of brain power, especially when there are many more unsettled and perplexing philosophical problems yet to be resolved.

Nevertheless, I would argue that many of us who at least have been students, if not yet teachers, would be hard pressed if asked to spell out in simple words the ideas contained in such ordinary concepts of education as teaching, learning, or subject matter. Yet these very concepts are basic to any intelligent thought or discussion about education. Furthermore, I believe that an explication of these ideas would invariably result in the unveiling of important nuances of meaning which we unconsciously assume in our discourse and in our actions as students or teachers. As a result, we would not only become more sophisticated and careful in their use, but we would also gain a deeper insight into education as a human endeavor. This is the point of the philosophical analysis of educational concepts.

DEFINITIONS OF EDUCATION

I do not mean to give the impression that few people ever try to *define* education. From A to Z, from Admirals to Zealots, we find many persons, both in and outside the field of education, who are not only ready to talk about education, but who are also most willing to offer their definitions of education. In fact, it is not *a* definition of education which is lacking. Part of the problem involved in talking and thinking about education is the variety of definitions and views of education offered to us on all sides. We are literally bombarded with a multitude of competing definitions which tempt us to choose among them, to mix an eclectic set of fragments from them, or even to reject them all and find *the* "real" definition of education for ourselves.

Under this barrage of definitions, a very crucial assumption is frequently hidden. That is, we assume that there is only *a* definition of education or *the* definition of education. We act as if we were searching for that definition much as a big-game hunter searches for an elephant, confident that he will recognize one when he sees it and net himself a most valuable trophy. But what if we are really more like a sincere but misguided centaur hunter who, even with a fully provisioned safari and a gun kept always at the ready, nonetheless will never require the services of a taxidermist? Could it be that *the* definition of education is more centaurlike than elephantlike? Is there such a thing as *the* definition of education?

Instead of directly attacking this last question, let us turn to an examination of the idea of definition itself. In his book, *The Language of Education*, Israel Scheffler discusses three types of definition: the stipulative, the descriptive, and the programmatic.[1] Al-

---

1   I. Scheffler, *The Language of Education* (Springfield, Illinois: Charles C. Thomas, 1960), Chapter 1.

though in practice these may not always be found in their pure forms, Scheffler ascribes certain distinguishing features to each.

A stipulative definition is one which is *invented* or, better, one which is given by its author, who asks that the defined term be consistently taken to carry this stipulated meaning throughout the ensuing discussion. One might, for instance, say, "Look, I know that there are various definitions and views of education currently in vogue, but in order to keep things straight, I shall use the word 'education' throughout my discussion [speech, article, book, etc.] to refer only to that social institution created and maintained by a society in order to perpetuate certain aspects of its culture through purposeful teaching and learning." This is a stipulation. It is saying, "This is precisely what I will mean by the word 'education', regardless of what others may mean."

The essence of a descriptive definition, however, is not a stipulative assertion that such and such will be *my* use of the term. Rather, such a definition purports to adequately *describe* what is being defined or the way in which the term is used. In effect, a dictionary attempts to provide descriptive definitions; thus, not infrequently, several definitions are given for a word, because many words have multiple descriptive meanings. However, the dictionary does not permit us to choose a definition arbitrarily; it provides us with the different ways in which a word is used in differing contexts. Consider the word "run," for instance. It has many definitions, each of which is appropriate only to some specific context. If John *runs* a footrace, we expect him to physically propel himself as fast as he can, whereas if he *runs* for president such a description of his activities seems quite inappropriate. Moreover, if Susan's stocking *runs* or if the colors in her painting *run,* we have two more different and noncompeting descriptive definitions of the word "run" exemplified by application to different contexts. In the first, "run" means an unsightly separation of woven strands, whereas in the second, we use "run" to mean a spreading and mixing of colors. Thus, there is not *a* descriptive definition of the word "run," but many definitions describing the appropriate uses of that word in differing contexts.

The stipulative definition of education offered above was also a descriptive definition, in that it referred to our use of the word "education" to describe that special institution created and maintained by a society in order to transmit aspects of its culture by means of purposeful teaching and learning. There can be no doubt that this definition describes *a* very broad use of the term "education," which ranges in proper application from the formal schooling which takes place in a complex society to the informal schooling of an aboriginal village, where a father teaches his son to make weapons or to hunt game. But this is only *one* of the descriptive definitions of education. The term can also be used quite appropriately in situations not characterized by purposeful teaching and learning. One example of such a context would be the autobiographical account of one man's "education" found in *The Education of Henry Adams* or, more generally, "education in the school of hard knocks" (education by means of experience rather than by purposeful teaching and learning). It would seem foolish to argue that the first definition is the true definition, since both usages are proper descriptions of what we mean by education in differing contexts. To stipulate that the first definition will be used throughout a discussion is not to legislate out of existence the second definition or any other proper descriptive definition. Stipulation of this sort is merely a device or convention for keeping things straight. Moreover, it seems that we should have little room for real disagreement over definitions which are descriptive, and, if we did, it should not be too difficult a matter to resolve them in some objective way.[2] After all, the objective description of anything is but an attempt to be true to what is in the public domain.

Why, then, we might wonder, do our current definitions of education lead to, or form the basis for, vehement disagreements over educational aims? Could it be that they are but competing stipulations? It hardly seems possible that we should have such quarrels over stipulations about how a term is to be used temporarily, but should it not be equally true that it would be foolish to argue over the correctness or "truth" of descriptions of how a term is *in fact* used in different contexts? An answer, I think, can be found in Scheffler's notion of the *programmatic definition,* a definition which tells us overtly or implicitly that this is the way things *should* be. Thus, one might define education as the development of mental powers, thereby implying that the curriculum should be totally directed toward intellectual development (not social or physical development) of students. To say what something *should* be is quite different from trying to say what it actually is or merely saying, "I'll use *this* to mean *it* for now." Definitions of education which are programmatic are frequently mixtures of the *is* and the *ought,* of the descriptive and the prescriptive.

Consider, for example, a definition that describes education as "the means by which a society attempts to develop in its young the capacity to recognize the good and worthwhile in life." Here we not only have the descriptive element of education as an instrument or institution of society, but we also have a program suggested. Implicit in this definition is the prescription or normative statement: "Educa-

---

2   See Scheffler's discussion of borderline cases in descriptive definitions: Ibid., pp. 18, 27–29.

tion *ought* to develop in people the capacity to recognize the good and worthwhile in life." This would give singular priority to a program of moral and aesthetic education, while saying little or nothing about what else education is or should be.

Now, on a moment's reflection, it should not be surprising to anyone that definitions of education frequently contain, either explicitly or implicitly, certain programs, norms, prescriptions, or values. After all, education is a human enterprise in which people attempt to do something in a purposeful, thoughtful, and careful way. Acting purposefully with some end or procedure in mind is, in one sense at least, holding that end or procedure as valuable, good, desirable, etc. Just as doctors try to cure their patients because they value health over disease, so educators try to produce open-mindedness in students because they value that quality over the closed mind. We could enumerate many other instances of the way in which certain values enter into purposeful human activities, but at this point that hardly seems necessary. Instead, let us turn back for a moment to the questions we left earlier regarding *the* definition of education.

With these ideas about types of definition squarely before us, it seems that, at the very least, our definitional question is ambiguous. In asking if there is such an animal as *the* definition of education, we might mean: Is there any such thing as *the* stipulative definition of education, or *the* descriptive definition, or *the* programmatic definition? Seen in this light, our question now really constitutes three questions. To recognize this seems to be a step in the right direction, for if someone were to answer "Yes" to the original question, we wouldn't know which question was being answered affirmatively.

We might do well therefore to examine just what an affirmative answer might mean in each case. In terms of a stipulative definition, an unqualified "yes" answer would seem foolish, for the very essence of stipulation is the freedom of pronouncement. Logically any definition could serve as the stipulated definition of education, and so here, obviously, a request for *the* stipulative definition of education either is out of place or deserves a negative response. (Unless, of course, a stipulative definition had already been given, and the request is merely to refresh the memory.)

But if the question is asked with the intent of seeking *the* descriptive definition of education, an affirmative response implying that there is one and only one true descriptive definition would be puzzling at this stage of the game, for we have already seen the possibility of multiple descriptive meanings of "education" for varying contexts and purposes. But let's say that we could produce a simple definition (such as "education is learning") which would fit all appropriate contexts. Such a definition might possibly satisfy all, but by the same token it would say very little to anyone. (One can learn to be a burglar as well as to be a lawyer, or learn from experience as well as from a teacher.) In essence, then, we might be able to produce a simple, all-purpose descriptive definition of education. It may very well leave us cold, though, for such a broad, indiscriminate, and non-evaluative use of the term can hardly be very useful.

Rather, and this is the intended upshot of this discussion, a search for *the* definition of education is most probably a quest for a statement of the *right* or the *best* program for education and, as such, is a prescription for certain valued means or ends to be sought in educating. In my view, asking for *the* true programmatic definition of education is very much like asking, "Which is *the* true religion of man?" or "Which is *the* true flavor of ice cream—chocolate or vanilla?" I juxtapose ice cream and religion not to be irreverent, but merely to indicate the range and complexity of value questions in education. Some, like ice cream flavors, are pure and simple preferences of taste, while others, like religion, are firm beliefs around which some grounds and rational superstructures have been developed. To argue that the school should teach good manners is closer to the "ice cream" end of the continuum; to advocate the school as the prime teacher of democratic values is closer to the "religion" end. Whether students should be taught to rise whenever the principal enters the room is a less crucial value decision than deciding whether or not they should be taught to be responsible and loyal democratic citizens. While there can be no doubt that decisions of value must be made in education, and that some will be extremely crucial decisions, to make them *by definition* seems hardly to be the most rational approach. Important questions of value require critical and careful judgment, not merely solution by definitional fiat.

VALUES IN EDUCATION

Notice that we have unearthed a new area for examination—the controversial area of values and aims in education—while the meaning of "education" has been left unresolved. It is important for the reader to understand clearly at the outset what we will be doing in this book. Thus far in this chapter, we have been dealing with conceptual issues and not with empirical or evaluational ones. In the remainder of this book, just as we attempted to unravel what it might mean when someone asks for a definition of education, we will demonstrate and use some philosophical techniques for getting at the meaning of a number of basic educational concepts. We will not necessarily be concerned with finding *the* answer to substantive problems. In this way, our personal values or the facts of the case often will be out of place in our examination of educational ideas. What will always be relevant to our philosophical concerns, however, will be questions of meaning.[3]

In sum, this book is an attempt to get at the meaning of education by carefully examining some of the ideas attached most closely to the concept of education itself. Thus, no single definition will be offered as *the* definition of education in these pages; rather, we will strive to pull apart some major aspects of the conceptual framework of education to get a better look at it. A definition of a clock as a timepiece may be helpful, but if you really want to get a working understanding of clocks, a careful disassembly of a clock and a diligent examination of each component's function would certainly be more instructive. As we already have seen in our discussion of definitions of education, tightly bound to the general idea of education is the idea of value. In fact, in his "pulling apart" the idea of education, R. S. Peters argues:

> [The concept] 'education' relates to some sorts of processes in which a desirable [valued] state of mind develops. It would be as much of a logical contradiction to say that a person has been educated and yet the change was in no way desirable as it would be to say that he had been reformed and yet had made no change for the better... something of value should be passed on... the truth is that being worthwhile is part of what is meant by calling it education....[4]

In one sense, Peters' claim is quite true. Part of the mental baggage carried along with the idea of education is the notion that education is valuable and that what people are to learn is valuable. We teach reading and writing because we believe it to be valuable for young people to learn to read and write their own tongue. In our society, we provide an education for medical doctors but not for witch doctors, because we regard a knowledge of medicine to be valuable, while holding a knowledge of magic spells and incantations to be of no medical value. One could obviously go on with such a list of examples. There is truth in Peters' claim, at least to the extent that those who advocate some type of education are, in effect, also impli-

---

3   Locating the proper domain for philosophical analysis is always difficult for the beginner. Those who may have some problem doing so after reading this chapter might find the section in the epilogue entitled "Locating the Field of Play" helpful in this regard. See pages 93–97.

4   R. S. Peters, *Education as Initiation* (London: Evans Bros., Ltd., 1964), pp. 15–18. This printing was a limited edition, but a version of this work appears in R. Archambault, ed., *Analysis and Education* (New York: Humanities Press, 1966).

citly saying that that type is desirable and/or valuable. To advocate liberal or technical education is to say that these types of education are valuable. Even when no specific type or goal-oriented adjectival form of education is being advocated, "education," like "love" and "mother," is blessed with a positive aura.

Granted all of this, it should not be difficult to see that there is another dominant sense of the ordinary notion of education which is not so value laden. If I refer to German education in the 1930s under Hitler, I am not necessarily assuming that something worthwhile was going on or that something of value was being passed on. Indeed, it would not be illogical to hold that the German youth of that period were educated quite successfully and yet also hold that German education under the Nazis did not produce a valued and desirable state of mind in the youth of Germany. In simple terms, then, there are contexts in which the term "education" does not carry with it the notion of value. I may decide to study Chinese education, of which I now know little or nothing, and yet not commit myself in advance to the proposition that there must be something of worth being passed on in Chinese schools. In fact, I may decide after completing my study that the forms and goals of Chinese education are all wrong, and yet there would be no contradiction in saying that the Chinese were being educated, while at the same time holding that much of what they were learning was most undesirable.

Notice, however, that if I were the Chinese minister of education or, in our first example, the Nazi minister of education, and if I were to advocate a special form of national education, then it would be most probable that I would also believe that form of education to be desirable. Hence, we might say that there is a dominant *subjective* contextual use of the term "education" in which an assumption of positive value exists, but also that there is an *objective* contextual use in which neutrality towards the value of education may be maintained. Thus, Peters' claim is only half true, and so it will be possible for us to deal with the idea of education and such auxiliary notions as subject matter and learning without first committing ourselves to some value(s).[5]

---

5   I should like to make it clear here, however, that the practicing educator cannot remain neutral. This is the important force of Peters' claim. Value decisions are integral to educating and, as I hope this book will be educative, I have not refused to commit myself to certain values. Although most analytic philosophers of education attempt to remain neutral in their writings, I cannot do this as a practicing educator. Nevertheless, I do see "value" in assuming the neutral approach while delving into educational ideas as deeply as possible *before* trying to decide or argue some positive or negative value position. This will generally be my approach in this book.

A pause for perspective seems to be in order before we go on to questions about aims in education. I have tried to show that conceptually we can get at the idea of education without first defining the term or commiting ourselves to some particular programmatic view of education or, indeed, without even assuming, as Peters does, that the very meaning of education itself must include the notion of positive value or worth. But more than this, consider the type of neutrality which has been maintained thus far. First we explored some ideas about the definition of education and then looked at the notion of the implicitness of positive value commitment in the subjective contextual use of the term "education." We might very well have dealt quite differently with these same topics. We could have carefully built a complex definition of education which was a mixture of the descriptive and programmatic. We also could have supported Peters' claim and gone beyond it to show what is of most worth in the context of American education in the twentieth century. Some readers would have considered this a much more productive use of time. But notwithstanding their judgment, it is of most importance to the next topic—aims in education—that I put squarely before the reader what has and has not been done. We examined ideas central to any search for *the* definition of education by using the perspective of Scheffler's distinctions between three types of definition, but *the* definition was not provided nor was such a search even undertaken. It was not, "What is *the* definition of education?" but the prior question, "Does it make sense to seek *the* definition of education?" that was considered basic. In dealing with the relationship of education to values by examining Peters' claim, we did not even seek to determine "What is of value in education?" but rather to deal with a prior conceptual question which asked, in effect, if it makes sense to assume that our ordinary idea of education always carries with it a commitment to positive value. Sometimes such prior questions are called *metaquestions* by analytic philosophers, but knowing what they are called is not as important here as understanding what kind of questions they are. We will call them **prior questions**[6] or **conceptual questions** in this book to distinquish them from factual or valuational questions.[7] They do not ask for the facts of the case, nor do they require some value decisions to be made. **They are questions**

---

6   As noted in the preface, I will highlight the introduction of a new technique or strategy with **boldface** type.

7   A very rich and thorough discussion of this distinction is provided by John Wilson in his useful book, *Thinking With Concepts* (Cambridge: Cambridge University Press, 1963). See especially pages 1–16. I have tried to summarize his major points in the epilogue under the topic "Locating the Field of Play."

of meaning and, as such, generally are nonsubstantive; that is, they do not deal with the factual or valuation substance of the topic. Rather, they are questions that seek conceptual clarity before commitment to the substantive exploration of a topic.

Thus, no definition was given for education, although ideas about education and definitions were examined. Nor was there any substantive decision on what is of value in education. Rather, ways were provided of examining the ideas that stand behind these substantive educational questions and topics. As we turn now to discuss the topic of aims in education, we will not ask what is *the* aim of education or which aims of education are more appropriate than others, or even what aims are utlimately of value. Rather, we will look more closely at the notion of aim itself and follow Peters' lead in asking the prior question, "Must an Educator Have an Aim?"[8]

AIMS OF EDUCATION

Of course, before we can directly attack Peters' question, we must have some idea of what it means to have an aim. John Dewey recognized, as we all should with but a moment's reflection, that "Education as such has no aims. Only persons, parents, teacher, etc. have aims, not an abstract idea like education."[9] In simple terms, having an aim is having some purpose or goal *in mind,* and it is in this ordinary sense that we speak of the aims or ends of education with the implicit assumption that these are the purposes or goals which certain *people* believe to be educationally desirable or valuable. Thus we speak of education for democracy, for citizenship, for intellectual discipline, for emotional maturity, for the Good Life, for the liberally educated individual, etc. In doing so, we are looking toward some formulation of the result of schooling or for some guiding purpose to provide a cohesiveness to the pattern of schooling. But if education is to have an aim, it must be we who give aim to it and not it that gives aim to us. Aims of education are to be found in the minds and hearts of people, and not in a mindless social institution called "education." But then, what can we make of Peters' question, "Must an educator have an aim?" Surely he is not asking if educators do have aims. Of course they do. Rather, he is asking if having an aim is an integral

---

8   This is the title of one chapter in R. S. Peters' interesting collection of essays: *Authority, Responsibility and Education* (London: George Allen and Unwin, Ltd., 1959), pp. 83–95.

9   John Dewey, *Democracy and Education* [New York: Macmillan 1916 (1961 paperpack edition)], p. 107. In his chapter on aims, Dewey does an admirable job of analysis of the concept of aim as end-in-view, which he distinguishes from mere results of actions.

and necessary part of our conception of being an educator. More directly, he is asking, "Can anyone be an educator without having an aim?" In my reading of Peters, it seems to me that he implicitly answers this last question affirmatively. And yet if I am correct about his answer, then we have a rather sticky puzzle before us, for it would seem at first blush that acting as an educator would minimally involve acting with some educational aim in mind—but Peters intimates that this isn't necessarily so.

The key to understanding Peters' suggestion that an educator need not have an aim is to be found in his restrictive use of the term "aim." Peters, quite appropriately to my mind, adopts the ordinary use of the term "aim of education" to designate a broad general objective much like those mentioned above. Traditionally, educators have felt that the final goal, the end product of the educative process, must be clearly seen and precisely defined before one can intelligently select the appropriate means to attain the desired outcome. Thus we are offered education for citizenship, moral character, and so on. But Peters attacks this general assumption that one cannot act or make decisions without first having a vision of what he is *ultimately* after. And he goes even further, suggesting that the idea of a means-end relation is not relevant when we speak of these ultimate aims of education. In doing so, however, Peters does not deny another dominant sense of the term "aim," which merely refers to acting with some immediate purpose or goal in mnd. Thus a kindergarten teacher may well have (and, indeed, *needs* to have) some immediate and concrete aim (purpose, goal, end) in mind, such as getting the children to learn the alphabet, without which he or she could hardly be called a teacher. Imagine such a teacher answering the question, "What are you trying to get your students to learn?" by saying, "Why, nothing at all. I have no purpose in my teaching. I don't try to get them to learn anything specific. I have no aim."

I am fond of quoting Dewey on this point, for I feel that he is most correct when he says that "acting with an aim is one with acting intelligently." In this general sense of "aim," we all have aims in our daily activities, and whether we succeed or fail in attaining our immediate aims, we can usually answer a question regarding our purpose for action by referring to our aim or end-in-view. I can think of no human activity that I would be willing to call intelligent which is devoid of some referent to an intended consequence, some direct or immediate aim.

But obviously, Peters is neither saying nor intimating that educators do not act intelligently, nor is he saying that they do not need aims in this simple and ordinary sense. Rather, he directs his attack at the first sense referred to about—*"ultimate* aims of education"—which we might hereafter refer to with a capital A for convenience. According to Peters, these ultimate Aims in education suffer from a major defect: "These very general aims are neither goals nor are they end products. Like 'happiness' they are high-sounding ways of talking about doing some things rather than others and doing them in a certain manner."[10] In effect, Peters argues that the very vagueness of these Aims does not allow them to serve as goals or ends in the same way as do such concrete and/or immediate goals as getting a group of students to learn the alphabet. Alphabet cards or pencil and paper are directly relevant to the task of learning the alphabet, but what, one might ask, has the learning of algebra, science, or composition to do with the attainment of moral character, the Good Life, or some such other general Aim of education? The direct relevance of these latter subjects to some Aim is not as clear as that of the use of alphabet cards to the aim of learning the alphabet. In fact, it is Peters' contention that arguments over Aims are more often disagreements over the way things are to be done than over what final outcomes are desirable. Could you imagine the educational traditionalist saying that he did not want young people to become responsible, well-adjusted citizens of our democracy, or the progressive saying that he did not want young people to fully develop their minds and moral sense? When we think of the stereotypes of progressives or traditionalists in education, do we not see that much of the difference between them is in how they perceive the proper procedures for teaching and learning, rather than in their general Aims? This is the force of Peters' admonition that, "The crucial question to ask, when men wax enthusiastic on the subject of their aims, is what *procedures* are to be adopted in order to implement them. We then get down to moral brass tacks."[11] And this is the key to seeing what Peters offers the educator in place of having to have a broad, comprehensive vision of the product of education. For Peters, ultimate aims serve properly not as goals to be pursued, but as sources for drawing out principles of procedure to be heeded when pursuing immediate aims as goals. He suggests that such "principles of procedure" are exactly what one needs in making intelligent decisions about immediate goals and ways of teaching and learning. For Peters, the educator can operate much like Oakeshott's political man sailing in the "ship of state" without "starting place nor appointed destination

---

10   Peters, *Authority, Responsibility and Education* (London: George Allen and Unwin, Ltd.), p. 86.

11   Ibid., p. 94.

[where] the enterprise is to keep afloat and on even keel,"[12] not to *finally* get here or there, to the port of "Moral Character," the "Good Life," the "Well-Rounded Person," or some other exotic utopian heaven on earth.

We have spent some time with Peters' ideas about "Aims in education" for two reasons. First, his discussion (which we have here only in capsule form) is a fine example of the philosophical approach to educational inquiry which we have been following thus far. Peters does not offer us an Aim or a set of Aims to adopt as goals, and even though he offers us the idea of using "principles of procedure," we are given no specific principles to follow. Thus, Peters clearly exemplifies the stance of **neutrality** as well as the technique of asking revealing prior questions. Moreover, and this is the second reason, we see one typical result of asking a prior question: **making distinctions** useful to our understanding of education in its full complexity. Just as the distinctions between stipulative, descriptive, and programmatic definitions helped us to see more clearly the various possibilities for defining education, so, too, the distinctions between aims and Aims enables us to look more critically at a central and deeply entrenched educational idea which is seldom questioned and thought about analytically, although it is often preached and quarreled about substantively. If Peters is correct, the crucial and telling features of any type of education are the procedures adopted, not the Aims espoused. But even if he is wrong, we have had put squarely before us a most central aspect of education—the *manner* or *way* in which education is to be carried on. It should take no great insight to see that no matter what Aim one might adopt and value most highly, be it "responsible citizenry," "intellectual development," "moral character," or any other such desirable state, what happens in the classroom—the *way* we educate—will be a most crucial factor in determining the results. Making relevant distinctions helps us to see this more clearly.

In the chapters that follow, we turn to consider and use the tools of analysis on such concepts as subject matter, teaching, and learning. Focusing on these concepts will bring us to the heart of the educational enterprise, in that they are used to formulate, theorize

---

12   M. Oakeshott, "Political Education," reprinted in Scheffler, ed., *Philosophy and Education,* 2nd ed. (Boston: Allyn and Bacon, 1966), p. 342. In a footnote on this same page, Oakeshott answers his critics who ask, "Why travel if there is no prefigured and final destination?" with a very thought-provoking reference to science, poetry, art, and other human pursuits which have no ultimate and final goal, but nonetheless are still considered worthwhile "journeys" to take while sailing for no "final destination."

about, and advocate various educational procedures. Before we take them up, however, we should try to pull together the dangling ends of our discussion thus far.

This chapter has focused on two concerns, one substantive and one procedural. I have tried to introduce the reader to some of the substance of contemporary analytic inquiry into the concepts of education by pointing to the pioneering work of Israel Scheffler and Richard Peters. I have also tried to alert the reader to some aspects of analysis: prior questions, making distinctions, the neutrality of conceptual clarification, and the point of conceptual analysis as a search for clear meaning. Even though we have not settled any substantive issue regarding education, I now feel certain of two things: first, I am sure that I used the term "education" quite frequently in this chapter; second, I am sure that few, if any, of my readers had any serious difficulty understanding what I meant by the term *in each context of its use*, even though I did not define it. This should not be surprising to anyone, for by this time in our lives we have already mastered the standard uses of thousands of terms in the descriptive definitional sense, even though we may be very hard put actually to define each term. Clearly, we do not really have much trouble either recognizing "education" when we come across it or using the term in standard ways. Rather, our trouble begins when we seek a programmatic, value-laden definition while thinking we are seeking a description. I do not oppose programmatic definitions for education, for in at least one standard sense (the subjective contextual use), education does imply that something of value is passed on. Practically speaking, there would be no point to engaging in intentional education without some value commitment or some desired program being operative. Rather, the point in showing the centrality of programmatic definitions in educational discourse is to make one aware (and perhaps even wary) of "hidden" value commitments, so that decisions of value can be more easily recognized for what they are and so be more directly examined and intelligently dealt with.

Although we cannot actually educate without some value commitment (while we certainly can educate without a definition), we did point to a standard sense of the term "education" as used in some objective context in which neutrality, and, indeed, even final negative evaluation, is quite possible. It is in this neutral and objective spirit that we took on a discussion of the concept of aims in education.

In essence, then, this first chapter was directed at two immediate objectives. The first was to deal with the two questions: "What is education?" and "What are the aims of education?" By not directly answering these questions and by asking prior questions instead, we were able to make clearer just what it is that these questions pre-suppose. Thus, the second objective of this chapter was to introduce the novice to a philosophical way of thinking about education and educational ideas which puts clarity of thought before commitment.

In the following chapters, we shall not avoid the sense of what these two traditional educational questions seek. Fundamentally, both search for a broad understanding of education viewed as a most important and pervasive human undertaking. There are many fruitful ways to gain such an understanding. A close analysis of some of the central concepts of education can contribute significantly to a general understanding of education as an intentional enterprise. To this end the remainder of this book is directed.

The disciplines and subject matter

2

We have seen that the term "education" is used in many different ways and yet is generally understood without definition in differing contexts. In the last chapter, however, one standard use of the term was omitted. We did not have occasion to use "education" to refer to a field of scholarly study or a subject that is studied at a university or teacher training school. If it had been used in such a context, I expect that my readers would recognize this particular and familiar use of the term. Like the term "engineering," we use "education" to refer not only to some specific activity or process in which people actually take part, but also to refer to the *study* of that activity or process. As such, "education" is taken to be a subject for study, just as history, chemistry, or mathematics is. But there is far from universal agreement on just how much the subject of education is like history, chemistry, or math. This question of similarity is usually expressed in some such form as, "Is education a discipline?"

In this chapter, we examine this question more closely, not in order to find an answer to it, but because it will allow us to illustrate a number of the analytic techniques already identified. In addition, it will serve to introduce the reader to the first of three basic analytic strategies for clarifying concepts to be dealt with in this book—the generic-type analysis. In fact, I would hope that the "Is education a discipline?" question, which bothered educators some years ago, would not *now* be a burning issue for readers. It's very difficult to focus one's attention on a strategy being employed when one is simultaneously pursuing a volatile substantive issue. And, the whole point of this "discipline" discussion is to introduce techniques and strategies, not substance. Our subsequent treatment of the concept of "subject matter," however, will return us to a dual focus by intro-ducing the strategy of a differentiation-type analysis and also by probing the concept for useful educational clarification.

We will proceed by first doing some preliminary groundwork and scene setting by way of asking prior questions and examining defini-tions and distinctions. Then, we turn to the direct use of the generic-type analysis itself. Model cases of disciplines will be tested against the features of nondisciplines in an attempt to clarify the generic features of those subjects privileged to be called "disciplines." In other words, we shall seek to find out what makes a discipline a disci-pline.[1]

EDUCATION AS A DISCIPLINE

Is education a discipline? If we merely mean by this question, "Is education taught as a subject at a university?" the answer is obviously "Yes." Surely those who concern themselves with the status of education as a subject of study cannot mean the question in this way. Rather, they feel the weight of recent historical tradition in which the older, more respected subjects are held to be *pure* or to be *really* academic subjects, while education is looked down on as unworthy of the honorific title of "a discipline" or "an academic subject." But, in point of fact, the highest academic degree, the Ph.D., is actually bestowed on those who complete a scholarly study of education, and so it seems that, in some sense at least, the "academic" status of education is recognized by the university community of scholars. For educationists with inferiority complexes, however, this seems not to be enough. In this century, they have

---

1   To keep the initiate's eye on the techniques and strategies of analysis, I have avoided dealing with the more interesting and more basic sense of the term "discipline," which refers to the fundamental forms taken by various groupings of human knowledge and all that such an analysis might have to say to crucial curriculum questions. For those interested in this dimension of the concept, the work of my colleague P. H. Phenix, *Realms of Meaning* (New York: McGraw-Hill, 1964) and of P. H. Hirst, *Knowledge and the Curriculum* (London: Routledge and Kegan Paul, 1974) provide full and cogent clarifications and are well worth reading.

given more direct attention to the question of whether education is a discipline[2] and have come up with three kinds of answers.

The first is an unqualified assertion that education *is* a discipline; evidence is offered to show how similar its subject matter or its study is to those subjects commonly recognized as disciplines. Others more cautiously answer the question with a qualified affirmative, usually indicating that the study of education has the makings of becoming a discipline if only the scholars of education would tighten their academic standards, collect and organize more data, and come up with better theories. Finally there are those who argue that education is not now, nor can it ever become, a discipline. They see education as a professional subject, such as medicine or engineering, which draws its basic ideas and techniques from those academic disciplines which are relevant to understanding and carrying on the practical business of educating.

Although the question of whether education is a discipline has sparked an interesting and, for some, an emotionally, morally, and psychologically crucial debate, let us avoid the heat of this battle for the moment so that we may ask a most important prior question which may throw some needed light on this debate and, more importantly, on the concept of a subject itself. Instead of asking if education or, indeed, any subject, such as home economics, accounting, or animal husbandry, is a discipline, let us ask, "What is a discipline?"

This is an obvious prior question and, as such, is one which many who concern themselves with our problem recognize and answer forthrightly with a *definition* of a discipline. Thus, for example, we find John Walton beginning a conference on "The Discipline of Education" with introductory remarks pointing to the need to be clear about the meaning of the term "discipline," so that the question of whether education is indeed a discipline can be properly answered:

> By discipline, I mean a body of subject matter made up of concepts, facts, and theories, so ordered that it can be deliberately and systematically taught.... A discipline, therefore, is a body of subject matter that is teachable....[3]

Since we have already dealt with the idea of definition, we should recognize the stipulative and descriptive aspects of what Walton offers as a definition of a discipline. But focusing on his definition for

---

2   See J. Walton and J. Kuethe, eds., *The Discipline of Education* (Madison: University of Wisconsin Press, 1963).

3   Ibid., p. 5. Reprinted by permission.

a moment should help us to find a more crucial prior question than the obvious definitional one, for, by definition, education as a subject is already a discipline for Walton, since it is a "body of subject matter that is teachable" and taught in many contemporary universities. But notice that any subject, such as home economics or automotive mechanics, also would be a discipline if we applied this criterion of "teachability" to it. Even such subjects as water skiing (which I understand is taught at some coastal universities in the southern United States) and flower arranging (which an undergraduate friend of mine received one credit for "studying" at a state university) would be disciplines according to Walton's definition. Thus this definition has no discriminatory force. It may define a subject in a very general way, but it hardly offers any way to distinguish disciplines from nondisciplines.

Perhaps Walton's difficulty stems from his failure to find *the* definition of a discipline, and we could expect to be able to solve this problem if we could only find it ourselves. However, instead of seeking *the* definition of a discipline (if there is one), we might do better to follow a technique developed in the last chapter and look instead at the *uses* of the term which are relevant to this topic.[4] The term "discipline" is used by academicians to refer to certain subjects, such as history, math, and physics, and not to others, such as home economics and water skiing. As a starting point, therefore, we seem to have a clear set of subjects whose status as disciplines or nondisciplines is not in dispute. The term "discipline" is clearly withheld from use when referring to such subjects as water skiing, flower arranging, animal husbandry, and home economics, even though these subjects are taught at universities and academic credit is given for their study. Of course, there is a grey area of use wherein some may refer to a subject such as education as a discipline, while others will refuse to apply the term.

Recognizing the existence of such a set of uses, we might take only the clear cases and try to find out what it is about one subset (the disciplines) which is different from the other subset (the nondisciplines). Thus we may be able to see more clearly what we assume about one subset which we do not about the other when we apply the term "discipline" in the way we ordinarily do.

This would make our prior question not, "What is a discipline?" (definitional), but rather, "What *criteria* or *standards* do we assume and apply when we distinguish the disciplines from the nondisci-

---

4   "Discipline," of course, is a term also used to refer to behavior and, while it may very well be the concern of a practicing teacher faced with a class of rowdies, this "behavior usage" is not our concern here.

plines in ordinary usage?" For there to be a difference between disciplines and nondisciplines, one set of subjects would have to have certain characteristics which the other set of subjects did not share. So let us try to isolate and identify some of these properties or characteristics.

We have already seen that to take the criterion of "teachability" will not do, for all manner of things are taught at schools and universities. But perhaps we can find a clue in the obvious fact that some subjects which are taught (such as animal husbandry or home economics) are technical and practical subjects, while the disciplines are generally considered to be theoretical and more remote from the everyday business of living. Certainly the natural sciences are heavily laden with theory and abstract ideas, and we might well say the same for the social sciences. Even the study of history and literature produces special theories and concepts.

But what of animal husbandry and home economics? Certainly these subjects are not devoid of theoretical considerations or abstract concepts. The concept of atomic weight in physics is no more abstract than the concept of budget in home economics. (In fact, the latter is probably more difficult to calculate than the former!) And while there certainly is a sense in which home economics is a practical subject, I have yet to hear of a physicist or sociologist who claims that his or her subject is totally impractical. In fact, many earn their living from "doing" physics or sociology, just as farmers earn theirs by "doing" animal husbandry (while the poor housekeeper earns little more than room and board for the "doing" of home economics).

So it seems that the characteristics of abstraction and theory are not firm enough to separate the disciplines from the nondisciplines, although there certainly are differing degrees of abstraction and theorizing which, while not precisely quantifiable, are generally recognizable. It would be most difficult to try to separate the Ph.D.'s in home economics or animal husbandry from their colleagues in physics or sociology solely by means of noting their lack of theoretical concern with the subject or its lack of abstract concepts. They may very well desire a practical result from their teaching (producing good farmers or household managers), but this hardly sets them apart from those who seek to produce well-trained physicists or sociologists who can apply their skills and knowledge in their respective vocations.

Perhaps, then, some other characteristics or criteria will give us a keener cutting edge for separating the disciplines from the nondisciplines. It might be claimed that the disciplines deal with unique, organized, and open-ended bodies of knowledge while the nondisciplines, by contrast, deal with a nonunique potpourri of already known and "settled" subject matter. There may be some merit in such a proposed criterion, for physicists do seem to deal uniquely with the structure and relationships of physical matter and their knowledge is tightly organized in theories and laws while still remaining open to new discoveries. But it would be difficult to deny a similar uniqueness to such subjects as home economics or water skiing, for, as subjects of study, they too have a singular focal point which allows one to judge just what knowledge is relevant to their domains of study. Moreover, I imagine that what is known in these two areas of study *is* organized and open-ended, at least in the sense that scholars in these fields do not assume that everything about home management or water skiing is fully and completely known already.

One might argue, however, that physics is pure, while home economics uses the facts, laws, the theories of the social and natural sciences and therefore is not unique in some pure sense. But math is used in both chemistry and physics, while basting is unique to cooking. History, on the other hand, freely uses the concepts and theories of economics, sociology, and political science in a way not so different from the use of biological, physiological, and chemical concepts in books on animal husbandry. Once again, our proposed criterion seems to foil us in our attempt to draw a precise line between the disciplines and nondisciplines.

Yet there may be some clear distinguishing mark which we have overlooked thus far. What of the notion that the disciplines posess a unique method for obtaining and organizing the knowledge relevant to each subject? Thus the historian operates differently from the chemist and the physicist operates differently from the sociologist. Each employs a special method for attacking problems and confirming results. Let's test this idea.

The chemist faces a problem: how to produce a synthetic rubber. He analyzes natural rubber and seeks chemicals with similar properties which have the potential to combine. He hypothesizes that a certain set of chemicals in a certain proportion put through a certain process of combination with proper heat and pressures will yield his substitute for natural rubber. He steps into his laboratory, weighs and measures his chemicals according to his calculated proportions, submits them to the proper heat and pressure, and . . . *Voilà!* Synthetic rubber!

The cook faces a problem: how to prepare a baked dish of meat, sauce, and vegetables with well-rounded nutritional qualities, good flavor, and sufficient quantity to feed four. The ingredients are chosen for their nutritional value, measured in terms of sufficient servings, subjected to heat and pressure, and . . . *Voilà!* Stew!

It would seem that a scientific approach, in its most general form, is shared by many subjects as a proper method for obtaining desired results. Yet if one were to claim uniqueness of method for each discipline, a similar claim for water skiing or cooking seems defensible.

But where are we then? Some fairly likely condidates for criteria to clearly separate the disciplines from the nondisciplines have been examined and found lacking in discriminatory power. Are there no unique characteristics for identifying the disciplines? If not, how do we recognize them and, moreover, how do we decide our first question about the status of education as discipline or nondiscipline if we have no clear idea of the appropriate distinguishing characteristics of each?

Certainly in our discussion not all the possible candidates for discrimination were examined, nor were those which were considered given really full and sympathetic treatment. Nevertheless, what has been demonstrated is that the concept of a discipline is at least an elusive one—certainly not easy to pin down with the precision necessary to clearly discriminate subjects ordinarily called "disciplines" from those which are not.

But perhaps the criteria for a discipline offered above were ill-chosen or poorly phrased because of my own belief that it is an historical accident that some subjects are called disciplines. I also feel that we unthinkingly continue this tradition by learning to use the name "discipline" only for certain subjects, much as we learn to call some clerics "priests" and some "ministers" until pressed to consider whether some never-called disciplines are "disciplines" or whether some priests are "ministers." Since this bias of mine may account for my failure to find a way to demarcate disciplines from nondisciplines, I feel obliged to offer the thoughts of the only other scholar I know who has asked this prior question in this same way, but who, unlike me, claims to have found a list of suitable criteria.

In his article, "On Becoming an Intellectual Discipline,"[5] in which it is argued that not only education, but other subjects may acquire the status of a discipline, Professor Shermis tells us:

A definition [of an intellectual discipline] satisfactory to all is probably not possible. Therefore, rather than defining the term, let us look at the admitted disciplines—liberal arts and the sciences—to see what it is that makes both of them intellectual disciplines. It will be seen, I believe, that both fields are

---

5   Sherwin S. Shermis, "On Becoming an Intellectual Discipline," *Phi Delta Kappan* 44 (November 1962): 84-86.

> *characterized by (1) a rather impressive body of time tested*
> *work, (2) a technique suitable for dealing with their concepts,*
> *(3) a defensible claim to being an intimate link with basic*
> *human activities and aspiration, (4) a tradition that both links*
> *the present with the past and provides inspiration and sus-*
> *tenance for the future, and (5) a considerable achievement in*
> *both eminent men and significant ideas.*[6]

With this more elaborate statement of five carefully phrased and thought-out criteria, we can easily see the "fit" of the recognized disciplines. Surely history no less than science, mathematics, and literature has its "body of time tested works," "suitable concep-tualizing techniques," a "claim" of linkage to "basic human activi-ties," a "tradition" linking "present with the past" which provides "sustenance for the future," and "considerable achievements in both eminent men and significant ideas." Here we well might have what we have been seeking—a sound set of criteria that point clearly to those characteristics which make a subject a discipline. But have we? Is the cutting edge of these noble phrases keen enough to separate the meat from the bone?

Let us try the subject of cooking, which is taught in school under the aegis of home economics, but which hardly seems to have that pureness of sublimity associated with an academic subject or "intellectual discipline." Surely cooking has a "rather impressive body of time tested works" (recipes), "technique[s] for dealing with [its] concepts" (basting, frying, broiling, baking, etc.), "a defensible claim to being an intimate link with basic human activities and aspirations" (eating and the enjoyment of food), a "tradition provid-ing inspiration and *sustenance*" (what need be said?), and a consider-able achievement in both eminent men (Chef Boy-ar-dee!) and signifi-cant ideas (pizza!). Alas, 'tis a foul deed done to so noble a list! But should the nobility of words keep us from demanding the precision of ideas? I hope not, for not only is the language of education filled with high-sounding but vague phrases which sway us away from clear thinking, but so is much of our discourse in other spheres pretending to knowledge.

So once again, unfortunately, we have not solved a problem, but rather opened it up to see how difficult it is. However, we may lay claim to something positive other than to the fact that characterizing a discipline is a most difficult, if not impossible, undertaking. By glancing back momentarily at our journey through the examination of the concept of a discipline, it should be apparent that we employed a new and valuable technique for clarifying ideas beyond the asking

---

6   Ibid., p. 84. Reprinted by permission.

of a prior question. In its simplest form, **we tested abstract ideas by means of applications to concrete examples.** Thus we took some ideas that seemed appropriate to the concept of a discipline and tried them out to see if they fit all recognized disciplines. In this way we sought those common elements of disparate subjects which make them sufficiently similar to one another to rate the same title. History is not mathematics, nor is physics literature, but we did not seek to find criteria to separate these from one another. Rather, we sought the common elements that make each of these a discipline.

But to have done only that would have put us in the position in which we found Shermis. Crucial to our application of ideas to concrete subjects to see if the ideas fit all recognized disciplines was our corresponding **use of counterexamples.** By taking those subjects recognized as nondisciplines, we were able to test the power of our criteria to separate disciplines from nondisciplines. The use of counterexamples showed us that our ideas lacked the keen cutting edge needed. The technique of example and counterexample will prove quite valuable in the discussions that follow, as we continue to probe the concepts of education in an attempt to make them clear and understandable.

Before we go on, it might be useful to give a name to the more general strategy used in dealing with the concept of a discipline, so that we may later distinguish it from other general analytic strategies which also employ the techniques of example and counterexample. Since the point of such an analysis is to try to identify the general or generic characteristics of a concept, we will call it a **generic-type analysis.**[7] The form which this type of analysis takes can

---

7   One of the best straightforward uses of a generic-type analysis is afforded by Harold Weisberg in his essay, "Tradition and the Traditionalists," in *Philosophy and Education,* 2d ed., ed. by I. Sheffler (Boston: Allyn and Bacon, 1966), pp. 349–357. Weisberg examines the notion of tradition as it is used in educational arguments to support the teaching of certain subjects. First he shows the difficulty in providing criteria for what is to count as tradition, and he then argues that appeals to tradition are generally hidden appeals to specific values or some specific tradition, because there is no *tradition* per se, but only a host of *traditions* from which one must choose. I highly recommend this essay both for its demonstration of the generic-type-analysis strategy and for the consideration of the substance of his argument, especially since the idea of passing on the "tradition" figures so heavily in educational thinking and debate over the curricular status of many subjects. Also see Wilson, *Thinking with Concepts* (Cambridge: Cambridge University Press, 1963) with its many examples of generic-type analyses and T. I. White, "The 'University Community' and Political Ends: A Critical Examination," *Proceeding of the Philosophy of Education Society 1974* (Edwardsville: Studies in Philosophy and Education, 1974), pp. 304–312.

be simply sketched, as can the strategy used in trying to achieve its purpose. **The prior conceptual question, "What is an X?" is asked and taken to mean, "What are the basic features which make an x (species) an X (genus) and provide the criteria for distinguishing X's from non-X's?"** In our demonstration analysis we recognized the need to ask the prior question, "What is a discipline?" and sought those features which make any recognized subject like history or math (species) a discipline (genus). **The basic move of the strategy is to begin by identifying standard cases of X and clear cases of non-X.** We used history, math, and physics as standards and home economics, animal husbandry, water skiing, and such as clear nondisciplines. **Next one identifies a basic necessary characteristic of X from standard cases,** as we did first by looking at the theoretical and abstract nature of the disciplines. **Then, one tests the power of the characteristic to distinguish X's from non-X's by the use of counterexamples.** We did this by showing that such nondisciplines as home economics and animal husbandry share these characteristics to some degree. **Keep, reject, or modify the characteristics in light of the test. Test additional necessary characteristics in a similar manner and reach some conclusion on the sufficiency of characteristics and the degree of clarity reached in identifying conceptually what makes an x an X.**[8]

THE CONCEPT OF SUBJECT MATTER

Although we have not settled the question of the disciplinary status for the subject called "education," nor even the prior question of identifying the discerning features of an academic discipline, it should be clear that we can continue our discussion of subjects and subject matter without definite answers to these questions. For we can speak neutrally of a subject as the name given to any body of knowledge, whether that body be large or small, highly organized or not, traditional or new, etc., and this neutrality will allow us to apply our ideas to any and every conceivable subject, past, present, and future. The same holds as we move now to our discussion of subject matter, the "stuff" of a subject. The question of whether this or that bit of subject matter is worthy of being taught, although an important practical educational question, will not be our immediate

---

8   Having four sides is a necessary feature of being a square. If a figure has less or more than four sides, it cannot be a square. However, having four sides is not a *sufficient* condition for being a square. Rectangles and parallelograms have only four sides but are not squares. For anyone wishing a fuller elaboration of this strategy, see the epilogue section on "Generic-Type Analysis," pp. 98–101.

concern. Rather, we will seek a clearer understanding of the concept of subject matter itself, so that we will have a firmer basis for making such value decisions and, more important for our purposes, a better understanding of another very fundamental educational idea.

Let's begin by placing the concept of subject matter in its educational context. It is generally taken that "subject matter" is the middle term in a three-term relationship: Someone (S) teaches something (x) to someone (P). We need not worry about whether S and P could be the same person, for we are concerned here with the ordinary educational context in which the term "subject matter" merely refers to something that we speak of teaching and learning. Nor should we at this point concern ourselves with the possibility of a teaching failure, wondering about a case in which S *teaches* x to P, but P fails to learn x. In the next two chapters, we look more closely at the concepts of teaching and learning and consider such problems there. But our focus here will be primarily on subject matter as the "stuff" of teaching and learning. However, just as with any relational concept, it will be impossible to treat it without some reference to those things with which it is related. To paraphrase Scheffler in his examination of *The Language of Education,* we cannot just teach children nor just teach subject matter, for we must teach children something (subject matter) and we must teach subject matter to someone (children).

In his essay on "Uses of 'Subject Matter,' "[9] Professor Henderson makes similar observations about the triadic relational quality of the concept of subject matter and goes on to identify and reject certain ordinary uses of the term "subject matter," while seeking a clearer formulation of the term which will be "theoretically and practically fruitful." We shall follow his lead for the moment, briefly summarizing his arguments so that we may find what, if anything, can be puzzling or controversial about so ordinary and easily understood a term as "subject matter." We shall also use Henderson to demonstrate another general analytic strategy, that of the **differentiation-type analysis.**

Henderson begins by arguing that "for a concept of subject matter to be fruitful, it should assist the teacher in at least three important tasks related to subject matter: (1) selecting subject matter for consideration in his classes, (2) organizing the subject matter so that there is some relation among its composite elements, and (3) evaluating the students' acquisition of the subject matter."[10]

---

9   K. B. Henderson, "Uses of 'Subject Matter,' " in *Language and Concepts in Education,* ed. by Smith and Ennis (Chicago: Rand McNally, 1961), pp. 43–58.

10   Ibid., p. 44. Reprinted by permission.

He then examines what he takes to be the three uses of the term "subject matter," pointing to and refining one of these uses as the most fruitful. In so describing and naming the ordinary uses of the term, Henderson is **analyzing the concept** of subject matter **not by pointing to its necessary features (generic-type analysis), but by distinguishing among its basic meanings (differentiation-type analysis).** The many distinctions we have seen already represent just such an attempt to specify conceptual differences between potentially ambiguous uses of a term.

Let us try to follow Henderson's complex argument. First, he identifies "subject matter" as the term is ordinarily used to refer to "concreta,"[11] the *things* which we speak of teaching or learning, such as *Silas Marner,* skeletal structure, the solar system, magnetism, etc. While conceding that this way of speaking about subject matter allows for *selection,* Henderson maintains that it is inadequate for considerations of *organization* and *testing.* For subject matter is not something concrete partaking of physical properties, nor does it make literal sense to speak of teaching the solar system or teaching *Silas Marner.* In effect he seems to be saying that we teach students *about* such things as the solar system or *Silas Marner,* but could not teach the solar system or *Silas Marner* anything at all. The final inadequacy of the concept of subject matter used to refer to "concreta," according to Henderson, is its omission of the abstract, for we do ordinarily consider abstract ideas and symbols as candidates for subject matter.

Next, Henderson points to that use of "subject matter" which refers to the "content of the conventional subjects," such as math, science, or history, and rejects this use as too narrow, because it fails to make room for new subjects as yet not even dreamed of or new theoretical ideas about subject matter (*viz.* viewing subject matter as "experiences"). Finally Henderson gets to "the third and *last* use of 'subject matter' which can be identified [as] that which refers to knowledge."[12] With certain refinements, he takes this use to be the most fruitful theoretically and practically. Thus, by means of a differentiation-type analysis, we find Henderson basically in agreement with the unexamined assumption most of us have, which is that, in the context of educating, the term "subject matter" refers to the "matter" of some subject or, more precisely, to those "bits of knowledge" which we have about some subject. The other "uses" of

---

11   Ibid.

12   Ibid., p. 47. (Italics mine. Henderson clearly only recognizes three dominant uses of the term "subject matter." In the critique which follows, I will point to a fourth dominant use unexamined by Henderson.)

the term are rejected on the grounds of being not as useful or fundamental as this one.

This brings us to a most crucial set of questions about knowledge
and subject matter. First, we should ask what constitutes knowledge
and what forms knowledge takes.[13] Second, we should guard against
narrowness in our singular linkage of subject matter to knowledge,
asking if some things that are not generally taken to be knowledge
are nevertheless taken to be subject matter or at least considered by
teachers as potential candidates for subject matter to be taught to
their students.

But before we get into these questions, let us follow Henderson's
discussion of subject matter as knowledge a bit further to see where
that may lead us. Taking his lead from Ryle's[14] distinction between
"knowing *how* and knowing *that*," Henderson argues that performative knowledge—knowing how to do things such as swimming, playing chess, riding a bicycle, etc.—admits to grades of accomplishment
as activities, but is incapable of being true or false. Accordingly, such
types of knowledge constitute a "kind of concreta, namely 'behaviors' [and hence are undesirable reference for the term 'subject
matter']," while verbal or propositional knowledge, which can be true
or false, is the more useful sense of the term. Thus Henderson rejects
performative knowledge as not being a fruitful and theoretically proper referent for "subject matter," narrowing the application of
"subject-matter-as-knowledge" to verbal knowledge only.[15]

We have now reached the point at which we may test Henderson's conclusion in two ways. At one and the same time, we can see if

---

13   To ask what constitutes knowledge is to become concerned about the
generic features of anything we would call knowledge and to ask about the
forms knowledge takes is to seek appropriate *differentiations* or *distinctions* amongst things we call knowledge and speak about knowing.

14   Gilbert Ryle, *The Concept of Mind* (London: Hutchinson's University
Library, 1949), *passim.* See especially the chapter entitled "Knowing How
and Knowing That." For those unfamiliar with this distinction, it may be
simply though superficially stated as a logical difference between knowing
facts or having information (that), and possessing *skills* or being able to
perform certain operations (how). The former (facts, *that*) may be true or
false (Columbus discovered America), while the latter (skills, *how*) are not
"true or false" (swimming, fishing), but are skills accomplished to greater
or lesser degree. (We shall deal with this distinction at greater length and
with more sophistication in the next chapter.) Henderson calls these
"cognitive" and "noncognitive" forms of knowledge, but to avoid a needless confusion, I will maintain a single consistant terminology for this distinction as it is used in this book.

15   Henderson does include, however, prescriptive and valuational *statements* in the sphere of verbal knowledge, although this is philosophically a
quite debatable and unorthodox move.

his conclusion meets the three criteria of selection, organization, and testing which he himself set down as most pertinent to a concept of subject matter, and also stand back from Henderson's argument to test by example and counterexample the fit of his view on subject matter with our ordinary ideas and assumptions about subject matter.

To avoid an awkward form of substitution in our preliminary statement of the teacher–student–subject-matter relationship ("S teaches x to P"), let us reformulate it to read "S teaches Px." Then we will not have the odd-sounding substitution, "S teaches *that Columbus discovered America* to P," but will be able to say with more grammatical ease, "S teaches P *that Columbus discovered America*" (or any other x we may wish to substitute). We should also be aware at this point that not just anything may be substituted for our x in this formula, for it is clear that we can make sense of some such statements as "S teaches P history," wherein a subject is our x, and not some subject matter. It will be incumbent on us, therefore, to specify what may and may not count as subject-matter substitution in some general way.

In effect, this is exactly what Henderson has done in specifying that only verbal knowledge is a proper substitute for x in this formula. Now, however, let us hold this type of subject matter up to Henderson's own yardstick of providing the teacher with a concept of subject matter useful in "selection, organization, and testing" of what is to be taught. Considering verbal knowledge as subject matter, we now know what to select from, but if both verbal and performative knowledge are considered as subject matter, we would equally well know which type our selection could be from (that is, from either or both types). As far as *what* to select is concerned, however, we have no more idea of *what specific* verbal knowledge to select in the first case than we do in the second. There is a most important difference between knowing from *which* categories to select and knowing *what* to select. Holding verbal knowledge as a fruitful concept of subject matter because it assists the teacher in the task of selection is only true in the sense that the teacher now knows what to select *from,* but not in the sense of knowing what *to* select, which is the crucial practical question in teaching. For a teacher of history of mathematics to know that selections of subject matter should come from the vast store of verbal knowledge of the field is not much help with the problem of selection. Much the same could be said for organization. What puzzles the teacher is not so much *what* needs organizing as it is *how* to organize the subject matter into its most teachable and learnable form.

Moreover, considering "selection" from another point of view, we might question the narrowness of Henderson's single selection from the realm of verbal knowledge, even while admitting, as we have above, that this store of knowledge in any subject field is almost boundless. Why should selection of subject matter be limited to verbal knowledge? Surely it makes as much sense to speak of S teaching P *how to* paint or do philosophical analysis as it does to speak of S teaching P *that* Columbus discovered America. We certainly talk and act as if we wanted our students to learn skills (or in Henderson's term, "behaviors").[16] It seems odd that the most theoretically fruitful concept of subject matter omits a large category of things that we act as if it were valuable to teach and learn! Taking a simple literal view of Henderson's position, we might be forced to say that while the history teacher has an abundance of subject matter to teach, the poor teacher of reading has little or no subject matter to get students to learn. If we are not to consider skills as subject matter, things to be taught to and learned by P, where in the educational scheme would we put such things?

Personally, I find it more fruitful to consider both facts and skills as subject matter and, in this very book, I am trying to teach some analytic skills to all you P's. Not only do I hope to acquaint you with the substance, the facts of what I and others think about certain educational ideas, but I am also trying to provide through description and example some analytic techniques, strategies, and skills which I hope will also be learned. If you learn that there is a technique of asking prior questions and another of using examples and counterexamples to pin down abstract ideas while performing generic- and differentiation-type analyses, but are unable to utilize these techniques, I would feel that you had not acquired the subject matter of this book. In fact, I would even prefer that the verbal knowledge of this book be forgotten if I could be assured that the skills and strategies demonstrated here were acquired, developed, and used by my readers.

But this is a personal diversion and we should get back to Henderson's criteria. Certainly one can test to see if the subject matter of verbal knowledge has been acquired and retained by students. We can ask P if he knows who discovered America, and, if he

---

16 In fairness to Henderson, I should make it clear that although he is unwilling to call performative knowledge "subject matter," he does not deny a place for the learning of skills in a school program. However, I find it odd not that we can teach skills and students can learn them, but that such teachable and learnable things are not considered subject matter in Henderson's scheme.

says Columbus, count our teaching a success. But we can also test his skill at reading or doing sums or solving geometry problems. Certainly skills are testable.

But all this is only to show that the criteria of "selection, organization, and testing" which Henderson provided us with can be met by performative knowledge or knowledge *how*, as well as by verbal knowledge *that*. There is, in fact, another generally recognized area of "things" which are neither *thats* nor *hows*, but which still seem to be legitimate candidates for subject matter.[17] We not only speak of S teaching P *that* Columbus discovered America or of S teaching P *how* to read, but we also talk of S teaching P *to* appreciate music or *to* be honest. When we speak of getting people to learn to appreciate art, we do not mean merely that they should learn some facts about art and acquire some skill at intellectually examining works of art. We ordinarily mean more than this, and that something more is our intent to ensure that our students do, in fact, acquire the disposition or propensity *to* appreciate art (to tend to seek out and take advantage of opportunities to appreciate art or to actually attain the state of an appreciation of art). Thus, most art- or music-appreciation teachers would feel that they had not succeeded if their students never used the facts or skills they acquired in the classroom in their lives or failed to achieve an appreciation of art and music.

Once again, this brief reference to the different kinds of things that are ordinarily taken to be subject matter points to the value of a **differentiation-type analysis. We clarify and thus make more useful a concept by pointing to the different basic meanings it has.** The strategy and form of this type of analysis can now be briefly described. **The form the prior question takes is "What are the basic senses of X?"** Thus, Henderson asked what are the different senses of the term "subject matter"? **The strategy is to seek examples from ordinary language which will display different uses or meanings of the term.** We noted that Henderson grouped as basic meanings for the term "subject matter" such things as (a) *Silas Marner,* magnetism, the solar system, etc. (concreta); (b) math, science, and history (conventional subjects); and (c) knowledge—while we identified facts, skills, propensities, and attainments. **The next move in the strategy is**

---

17   In his book, *The Conditions of Knowledge* (Glenview, Ill.: Scott, Foresman, 1965), pp.17–23, Israel Scheffler does a differentiation-type analysis which distinguishes "attainments" and "propensities" from propositional and performance-type educational outcomes. While other writers have also recognized these, it is Scheffler who deals with them most fully in this and in his earlier book, *The Language of Education* (Springfield, Illinois: Charles C. Thomas, 1960), see especially Chapters 4 and 5.

to look for those boundaries between different proper uses of the term. For example, verbal knowledge has the distinguishing mark of being capable of being true or false, whereas "skills" or knowing how, does not. These distinguishing marks are tested and refined by means of examples and counterexamples until a useful set of basic uses or meanings or types results.[18]

SUBJECT MATTER AS "VEHICLE"

In discussing "facts," "skills," "propensities," and "attainments" in this cursory way, I have tried to suggest that these all are certainly some of the kinds of things which we do, in point of fact, speak about in connection with teaching and learning. Thus, they quite legitimately seem to be potential candidates for consideration as subject matter. Now there may very well be problems in thinking of skills or propensities as subject matter, just as Henderson has pointed to the problems of taking concreta such as novels or astronomical bodies to be subject matter. Nevertheless, until such things are more carefully and logically examined, it seems foolish to limit to the purely verbal the sphere from which subject matter may be drawn, especially since we speak (and quite intelligibly, I might add) of teaching things that are outside the realms of verbal knowledge.

By thinking along the lines we have followed, we come now to a most serious omission in Henderson's discussion of the uses of the term "subject matter." Recall that Henderson recognized only three uses: as concreta; as the content of the conventional subjects; and as knowledge. But implicit in the way we have been discussing other possible candidates for subject matter is a fourth use, which is also a dominant standard use in educational discourse overlooked by Henderson and one which may provide us with a fuller view of the relationship between teaching, learning, and subject matter. I will call this the use of subject matter as *vehicle*.

It can be easily formulated by a small addition to what we already have as a basic schema: S teaches P*x, so that y*. Put into a concrete example, we speak of teaching someone the facts about slavery in the United States prior to the Civil War *so that* he will understand the current segregation problem, or we speak of teaching someone how to shift gears *so that* he may learn to operate a motor vehicle.

18   For a fuller elaboration of this strategy, see the epilogue section, "Differentiation-Type Analysis," pp. 101–103.

In this way we use the concept of subject matter (x) as a "vehicle" to get us to some goal (y). This usage is very natural to the idea of teaching as an "intentional activity."[19] When we teach, we are trying to get someone to learn something, very often for some reason. Granted, x may be y [or, in more concrete terms, we may just teach someone how to tie his shoe (x) so that he will know how to tie his shoe (y)], but in most cases our intentions of success far exceed the mere learning of some particular. In fact, given the formulation in which the *reason* for our teaching is made *ostensible* in the basic representation of the relationship between teaching, learning, and subject matter, we have what seemed to be missing when we discussed the inability of various candidates for subject matter to fully satisfy Henderson's three criteria of selection, organization, and testing. Given a y, we have a better guide for selecting and organizing our subject matter and a better idea of what to test for. Taking the example above of teaching the facts about the Civil War (x) so that our students can understand the current problems of segregation in the United States (y), we can see how this formulation comes closer to meeting the three criteria. There are many facts about the Civil War, but some are more relevant to our y (problems of segregation) than are others. Similarly, once we select those that are most relevant (it would be impossible to teach all the facts about the Civil War), then we have a guideline for organizing these facts in a way that will help us achieve our y. Finally, we can test not only for x, but also for what we were ultimately after, the y. We have a clearer picture of what we are after more immediately and sequentially and more remotely and finally.

This ordinary "vehicle" use of the term "subject matter" seems quite fruitful in putting more ideas about the teaching of subject matter into play, for it puts the activity of teaching into the intelligent and purposive context in which it belongs and allows for easy substitution of subject matter (what is to be taught), facts, skills, propensities, and attainments in either the x or the y category.[20] But in so viewing subject matter, we now find ourselves face-to-face not only with a broader relational view of subject matter, but also with some logical considerations about the concepts of teaching and learning. These will be our primary concern in the next three chapters.

19   See Scheffler, *The Language of Education*, p. 39 passim.

20   For an excellent application of this notion of subject matter as "vehicle," see Diane Benedict-Gill, "A Subject Matter Description of Moral Education," *Educational Theory*, 25, no. 2 (Spring 1975): 103–115.

Types of knowledge and teaching

3

We have seen that once we move beyond questions that ask what education is, we are able to focus more directly on the pulsating heart of the educational enterprise itself. Our discussion of subject matter has already brought us to a preliminary consideration of the essential aspects of the everyday business of educating—teaching and learning. In this chapter, we shall probe more deeply into the concept of knowledge. Once again, we will find it advantageous to talk about knowledge in the context of teaching and learning. Thus, in this chapter and the one that follows, our general purpose will be to examine and clarify some of the ideas that stand behind our ordinary notions about educating, while also more fully developing and describing the use of analytic techniques and strategies.

Although I tried to show in the last chapter that Henderson's view of subject matter as "knowledge *that*" was too limited, it certainly cannot be denied that much of what is taught and learned in formal educational situations is just this type of verbal or propositional knowledge. Therefore, we might profit from a fuller examination of this type of knowledge as it functions in the context of educating. Our central question will be: What constitutes successful teaching or learning of knowledge *that*? But we shall also deal with broader questions about the validity and purity of the various types of knowledge which, in the last chapter, we identified as potential candidates for subject matter.

REDUCTIONS OF TYPES OF KNOWING

We have already noted Ryle's distinction between "knowing *how*" and "knowing *that*," and, like Ryle, have generally taken these constructs to indicate two distinct forms of knowledge. Some, however, have gone beyond Ryle's treatment of this distinction and have raised questions about the validity of this distinction itself. We might do well, therefore, to begin our consideration of the concept of knowledge with a brief review of some of these discussions.

At the outset, it should be pointed out that one of Ryle's intentions in making this distinction was to debunk a rather pervasively held belief that all knowledge is fundamentally of a verbal or symbolic character, and that to know something is to be able to make appropriate statements about what is known. By pointing out that we commonly refer to people knowing *how* to do things and that this is different from their being able to describe such performances verbally, Ryle distinguished verbal knowledge from performative knowledge. Thus he was able to argue that if one knows *how* to swim, for instance, this does not imply or, indeed, necessitate that one have any verbal knowledge about swimming. And, alternately, acquiring verbal knowledge about swimming does not imply that one will then be able to swim. After pointing out this fundamental independence of verbal and performative knowledge, Ryle then chastised philosophers for giving their singular attention to knowledge of the verbal type and for treating it as *the* basic form of knowledge. (He might well have done the same for teachers!)

Be that as it may, Ryle's distinction was challenged in a most unique way by John Hartland-Swann.[1] In effect, Hartland-Swann argued that Ryle was quite right in chastising philosophers for focusing on verbal knowledge, but not because there was a basic difference between verbal and performative knowledge as Ryle maintained. Rather, Hartland-Swann argued that the general philosophical error lay in taking the wrong view of what knowledge basically is, for it seemed to him that Ryle had inadvertently shown that all knowledge

1   J. Hartland-Swann, "The Logical Status of 'Knowing That,' " *Analysis* (April 1956): 111–15.

was essentially performative.[2] More precisely, Hartland-Swann tried to show that knowing *that* parrots are birds or *that* George Washington was the first president of the United States was nothing more than knowing *how* to answer such questions as: What are parrots? Are parrots birds? Who was the first United States president? etc. That is, having verbal knowledge of some sort was having in one's possession that which is necessary to "perform" in certain ways in certain circumstances. In effect, he was arguing that verbal performances were not essentially different from any type of performance, and thus he came to the conclusion that all knowing is knowing *how* (performative).

Granting this conclusion that all knowing is performative, Jane Roland [Martin] nevertheless challenged Hartland-Swann's position, arguing that important distinctions between types of knowing (similar to Ryle's initial distinctions) would be obscured if one were to take knowing merely as performative.[3] In essence, she argued that certain performances required practice (e.g., swimming), while others did not (e.g., saying "George Washington was the first president of the United States"). Therefore, it seemed to her to be legitimate to maintain Ryle's distinction between knowing *how* and knowing *that* in terms of this "practice" criterion. Moreover, she also attempted to distinguish what we have here called "propensities" or "dispositions" from knowing how and knowing that. She did this by pointing out that, while the latter were both cases of *acquiring capacities* to perform in certain ways, in the case of "propensity" or "disposition" one needed to acquire something more than the *capacity* to act in a certain way, and that something more was the *tendency* to so act. To be honest is not just to know *how* to be honest, nor is it merely to

---

2   Since Ryle spoke of what we have been here calling "performative" knowledge as "dispositional" knowledge, and Hartland-Swann followed Ryle in this usage, I should point out that "performative" here follows my usage, not Hartland-Swann's or Ryle's. Since I have used the notion of disposition rather broadly to refer to the acquisition of propensities toward doing certain things in the last chapter, I have adopted the above terminology to avoid confusion. I suspect, however, that this footnote may create more confusion, but it is worth the risk for those who wish to pursue this topic beyond the brief consideration given it here. In addition, it may unwrinkle the eyebrows and prove soothing to those already acquainted with this literature.

3   Jane Roland [Martin], "On the Reduction of 'Knowing That' to 'Knowing How,' " in *Language and Concepts in Education*, ed. by Smith and Ennis (Chicago: Rand McNally, 1961), pp. 57–59. Once again it should be noted that Roland was considering the "dispositional" status of knowing (see the preceding footnote).

know *that* one ought to be honest. Rather, it is to *tend* to act honestly in appropriate situations, to be "prone" or "disposed" to so act.

Thus, in effect, Roland provided criteria to maintain the Rylian distinctions which we have been using and, moreover, also provided a way to separate propensities or dispositions from these two types of knowledge. But Roland did not stop there. She attempted to identify a distinct fourth type of knowing—e.g., "knowing how the accident happened," or "knowing how the motor works."[4] And beyond this she suggested, "A great many other 'knowing how' and 'knowing that' sentences, as well as 'knowing why,' 'knowing what,' and 'knowing about' sentences, remain to be examined."[5] The flood gates seem to be opened!

Indeed, Harry S. Broudy in his essay on "Mastery" identifies two (or possibly three) other types of knowing: "Knowing *what* or classificatory knowledge"; "knowing *why* . . . theoretical or explanatory knowledge"; and "conceptual knowledge" (knowledge *about*).[6] In our discussion of subject matter we have already noted the advantage of being able to clearly distinguish different types of knowledge from one another in the teaching-learning context. Yet one might become duly suspicious of this proliferation of types of knowing, especially if we were to continue on this tack, introducing such terms as "knowing *where*," "knowing *when*," "knowing *who*," etc., until all our conventional interrogatives have been used up!

At this point then, we may do well to pause for a moment to reflect on the differentiation strategy of distinguishing among types of knowing. Straight off, it seems that we could safely say that the search for types of knowledge is directed toward finding some logically basic sense or senses of knowing. The first move in this strategy often seems to be to take a variety of ordinary language references to instances of knowing, group them intuitively, and attempt to reduce them to some more fundamental type. This is what seems to prompt Hartland-Swann's reduction of Ryle's basic distinctions and Roland's attempt to maintain the logical purity of knowing *how* and knowing *that* as distinct types based on the "practice" criterion. But

---

4   Ibid., p. 65. We shall not examine this "type" here, but it will be considered in our discussion of explanation and understanding.

5   Ibid., p. 69.

6   Harry S. Broudy, "Mastery," in *Language and Concepts in Education*, ed. by Smith and Ennis (Chicago: Rand McNally, 1961), p. 77. The "knowledge about" label is my guess as to what Broudy might call "conceptual knowledge." I should also make clear here that although Broudy calls these "types" of knowledge, he maintains that they are or may be all "involved" in each other, and he is not very clear about whether or not they are logically distinct from each other.

if this is the strategy, then we might wonder why Roland posits a "knowing how the accident happened" type of knowledge and, moreover, why she does not attempt to reduce this to knowing *that*.[7]

After all, to know "how the accident happened" seems to mean no more than that one is in possession of certain verbal knowledge requiring no practice. That is, one may be said to "know" a singular relational proposition or some series of "thats." For example, one knows *that* the car skidded on the wet pavement and hit the telephone pole. Or we might say: He knows *that* the pavement was wet; *that* the brakes were applied too hastily and firmly; *that* the car skidded; *that* the telephone pole was in its path, *that* the car struck the pole; etc. Surely, to be in possession of knowledge about "how the accident happened" or "how the motor works" is to have "explanatory" knowledge (Broudy's "knowing why"), and whether we say, "He knows *how* it happened," "*why* it happened" or even "*what* happened" makes no difference with respect to the nature of the specific type of knowledge we have in mind (i.e., being in possession of explanatory knowledge).

Now, with respect to this brief treatment of "explanatory" knowledge, two important points should be noted. First, although the ordinary forms of language in which we express ourselves may be pregnant with assumptions leading to valid and valuable distinctions, we should not allow usage to befog the very ideas we are trying to clarify by means of a differentiation-type analysis. Thus, if we find in ordinary language usage clues to the identification of types of knowledge or whatever other things we might be looking for, we should never forget that the types themselves are our proper and primary conceptual focus, not the names we give them. Second, in thus briefly discussing the notion of an explanatory form of knowledge, we should not lightly dismiss the possibility that our proposed reduction to knowing *that* may not be adequate. That is, there may be room for argument that a series of *thats* form an explanation only if the series is connected by something more than another *that*; i.e., there may be also some pattern, a gestalt, an "appreciation" of the *way* in which the *thats* hang together and make sense to the individual. With respect to this latter point, we shall have more to say about explanation and understanding in the next chapter. Suffice it

---

7   Roland does consider such a reduction, but pulls up short of it by arguing that "knowing how the accident happened" really tells us nothing specific about what the knower knows while knowing *that* it was caused by icy conditions, say, does tell us directly what he knows. This seems to me to be an ordinary oddity of language rather than a point from which to make a logical distinction. Roland, "On the Reduction of 'Knowing That' to 'Knowing How,' " pp. 64–65.

here to suggest that if logical reductions to more basic types are to be
performed, they cannot be lightly undertaken.

Yet we might quickly dispose of two trival potential candidates
for distinct types of knowing which were mentioned earlier. Knowing
who (agent) or *where* (locus) seem to be but variations or, if one likes,
internal distinctions within the more basic and broad class of knowing *that*. To know *who* discovered America or *who* the first president
was seems no different than knowing *that* Columbus did and *that*
Washington was. Similarly, to know *where* London is or *where* Robin
is seems amenable to knowing *that* London is in England and *that*
Robin is in school. Likewise, knowing *when* (if it signifies a specific
temporal point in the past or future) is quite easily rendered as knowing *that* America was discovered in 1492 or *that* Parliament will con-
vene on September 12th.[8] Finally, to know *about* something seems
amenable to a similar form of reduction to a set of knowing *thats*.

Perhaps, however, we have overlooked an aspect of the differentiation strategy which might be more clearly brought out by looking at the participants we have considered in these discussions of
knowing. Although Ryle, Hartland-Swann, Roland, and Broudy are
all concerned with philosophical ideas about knowledge, Roland and
Broudy, as philosophers of education, are also concerned with the
relation of knowing to teaching and learning. This suggests the possibility that the philosophical moves of Roland and Broudy in dealing
with distinct types of knowing are guided no less by purely *logical*
considerations than they are by *pedagogical* considerations of the
relevance of such distinctions to the enterprise of educating.

Broudy's knowing *what* may be a good case in point. Logically
we might argue that knowing *what* ("classificatory" knowledge in
Broudy's terms) is ambiguous in that we might mean that to know
what an aardvark is is to know *that* an aardvark is a species of South
American anteater, while it might also be to know *how* to recognize
an aardvark when we see one or *how* to visually distinguish one from
a wild boar. Thus we might argue that logically, in some cases, knowing *what* is a performative type of knowing, while in others it can be
taken as purely verbal knowledge. But an examination of the logical
features of knowing *what* may not be what Broudy is concerned with
from a pedagogical point of view. That is, even though knowing *what*
may not be a logically basic type of knowledge, classification and

---

8   However, knowing *when to*, if there is any such animal, is a different
case altogether if it refers to some skill of judgment or strategy. For more
on this knowing, which might be taken broadly as general diagnostic skill,
see Broudy's discussion of judgmental skills in his essay on "Mastery," in
Language and Concepts in Education, pp. 73–75.

categorization are basic modes of arrangement for all types of formal subject matter. Thus, distinguishing something called "knowing *what,*" even if not a logically pure form of knowing, may nonetheless serve the educator well as a useful pedagogical distinction with respect to certain objectives of teaching and learning. Logical reductionism is not the only technique for making useful distinctions.

In short, with respect to the possible proliferation of types of knowledge, we might profitably distinguish between the search for logically basic types of knowing and pedagogically useful classification of knowledge types, always keeping in mind that, while the logical consideration may give us depth in understanding the type of knowledge we are dealing with, the business of education also has room for practical pedagogical considerations.

TEACHING AND LEARNING

It should be apparent from the above discussions of knowing "why," "what," "who," and "about" that many potentially identifiable pedagogical types of knowledge are reducible to knowing *that.* Thus one should hardly be surprised that much of what one finds in the classroom situation is the attempt to teach and have students learn what we have called here "verbal," as opposed to "performative," knowledge. This is not to say that skills are not taught, but is merely to suggest that a large part of what is taught and learned in the formal school situation is or could be reduced to the basic logical type called knowing *that.* It would therefore be to our advantage to spend what remains of this chapter focusing on "knowing *that,*" in an attempt to answer the question, "What constitutes successful teaching and learning of knowledge *that?*"

First, however, we might do well to settle some prior questions about the general notion of successful teaching itself by means of a blending of generic- and differentiation-type analyses.[9] In the last chapter, we noted Scheffler's recognition of the "intentional" use of the term "teaching," implying an activity undertaken in an attempt to get someone to learn something.[10] But Scheffler also recognizes, as should we, the "success" use of the term;[11] that is, implying an activ-

---

9   I call this a blending because, while it seeks the necessary general features of the generic concept of teaching, it does so by means of identifying base differentiations with respect to the concept.

10   Earlier (see p. 38), we used this idea to develop the vehicle sense of subject matter, which clearly separated what was intended to be learned from what was the intended purpose of that particular learning.

11   I. Scheffler, *The Language of Education* (Springfield, Illinois: Charles C. Thomas, 1960), pp. 42–43, passim.

ity that is undertaken to try to get someone to learn something *and* actually succeeds in effecting the learning. If we have been *trying* to get someone to learn something, we have been teaching (in the intentional sense), even if we fail to get him to learn. So it is possible to spend an hour, a day, or even a year, *teaching* Johnny how to subtract with the result that Johnny has not yet *learned* how to subtract. While some might be willing to consider such a case as very, very poor teaching, I imagine that others would not be willing to call this teaching at all, for they recognize only the success sense of teaching, in which teaching logically implies learning. But then what sense can we make of an ordinary example of a typical classroom situation? Suppose that a teacher, having spent the day "teaching" (intentional sense) a class of thirty children how to subtract, finds at the end of the day that, while twenty-nine are able to subtract, one is not. Are we to say that no teaching has gone on here because success is not 100 percent complete? Do we not, in fact, recognize that even superb teachers (whom we willingly call teachers) have some students who fail to learn what they teach? Clearly, teaching is an activity *aimed* at success (as well as one that is frequently successful), but, just as with the skillful doctor who occasionally loses a patient, so too teaching cannot guarantee (or imply) success, for success is only one of two possible outcomes of an effort to do something. To quote Scheffler, "Whether success is attained depends on factors outside one's trying: the [whole] universe must cooperate."[12]

Clearly, then, there seems to be a good case for recognition of both an intentional and a success sense of teaching. In what follows, this distinction will allow us to specify in each context the sense in which we are talking about the logic of the term "teaching." Scheffler himself utilizes these distinctions to great advantage in his discussion of a comparison between teaching and telling.[13]

Now let us try to apply the success and intent senses of "teaching" to the formula developed in the previous chapter. Quite simply, if S teaches P x (intentional sense), we have no implication that P has learned x. Similarly, if we say that S teaches P x (in the success sense), we are implying that P has learned x. But now let us try the "vehicle" notion of subject matter which we claimed made a place for

---

12   Ibid., p. 68.

13   Ibid., Chapter 5. Using the success sense of teaching, Scheffler skillfully argues that teaching *that, how,* and *to* does not imply telling *that, how,* or *to,* and alternately that success in telling *that, how,* or *to* does not imply success in teaching *that, how,* or *to.* I recommend this discussion for two reasons. First, it is an excellent example of analytic technique and, second, it forces consideration of the differences between informing, telling, or mere lecturing and teaching.

intent in our schema. If S teaches P x so that y, and we consider this to be the "intentional" use of teaching, then we do not imply that P has learned x or that y has been achieved. We may try to get P to learn how to swim (x) so that he will not drown (y), but we may succeed or fail in terms of either x or y or both. If, however, we use the success sense of "teach" in this formula, then minimally we can say that P has learned x, but the question of whether y will also result is open unless y is the same as x. That is, we may succeed in teaching P how to swim, but this does not guarantee that P will not drown.

Too often, I suspect, teachers assume that if P learns x, then y is also accomplished. It should be clear from this discussion that this is a very dangerous assumption. It may very well be that P has learned how to read (x), but does not like to read (y), or S may successfully teach P the relevant facts about slavery (x), but P may not understand the current problems of segregation (y). The relationship between immediate and more remote success in teaching seems to be even more tenuous and more easily overlooked than that between immediate intent and immediate success. Success in x but failure in y may result for many reasons, not the least of which is a false assumption about the necessary relationship between x and y. Certain facts about slavery may indeed be relevant to understanding the current problems of segregation in the United States, but merely learning these facts does not ensure that a person will also thereby attain an understanding of those problems.[14]

In any case, it should be clear that the concept of teaching is a rich one, with a complex logical structure. By means of a blending of differentiation-type and generic-type analyses identifying the essential features of teaching as a human activity with the intent to bring about learning, we have also been able to consider the logical possibilities of success and failure. Two additional analytic techniques have been demonstrated directly in our discussion. First, we should note the **use of concrete examples (not just counterexamples, but as positive instances) to bring abstract ideas down to earth.** This is an important as well as a pervasive philosophical technique. Second, **by providing a simple, formula-type schema of related concepts, as we did above with S teaches P x so that y, we create an economical way to cover a lot of logical and conceptual ground. Such a relational sketch not only gives us deeper insight into the concepts involved,**

---

14   We shall examine the phenomenon of understanding in greater depth in the next chapter. Questions about the "understanding" of x or y by P are questions about a very sophisticated learning outcome and, as such, demand fuller treatment than can be given here.

but also allows us to locate more easily logical possibilities and practical problems in that conceptual domain.[15]

TEACHING KNOWLEDGE *THAT*

Given the above general analysis, we can now turn to the narrower question of what should count as a case of successful learning and teaching of some knowledge *that*. Such a task is more difficult than it may first appear, however. For instance, I am sure that one could teach someone and have the person learn *that* the planets in our solar system travel in elliptical orbits. But what if our someone (P) is a child for whom the words "planet," "solar system," "elliptical," and "orbit" have no meaning? Even if P would reply properly to the questions: "What do you know about planets?" or "What have I taught you about planets?" with the words, "Planets in our solar system travel in elliptical orbits," we may hesitate in attributing knowledge *that* to P, or even to say in a very important pedagogical sense that P has learned *that* the planets in our solar system travel in elliptical orbits. Obviously, on the one hand, we are disturbed here by the "parroting" sense[16] of *learning* and by the felt need that whatever we say someone *knows* must in some minimal way "make sense" to that person or "be understood" by that person. On the other hand, we do use the words "learn" and "know" in reference to just such parroting cases. We say a young child has learned or knows the "Pledge of Allegiance," even though, on close inspection, the pledge might come out as a pledge of allegiance to the "United *Steaks* of America!" But we may ask what *type* of learning or knowing we really have in such cases.

Granted, it may fit the form of learning or knowing *that* x (the Pledge case does not quite seem to), but if the proposition x has little or no meaning to the individual—is, in effect, a set of nonsense

---

15   It is important to recognize that the concept of teaching also can be attacked via the strategy of a differentiation-type analysis by marking off differences between such attempts to bring about learning as conditioning, indoctrinating, propagandizing, training, and so on. One of the most readable and most successful attempts at this kind of analysis can be found in Thomas F. Green's "A Topology of the Teaching Concept," *Studies in Philosophy and Education* 3 no. 4 (Winter 1964–65).

16   See the discussion of this parroting sense by A. Castell in "Two Senses of Learn," University of Oregon *Curriculum Bulletin* 2 (1964): 9–17; and a further discussion of this sort of problem in P. Komisar's "More on the Concept of Learning," *Educational Theory* 15 (July 1965): 230–239. Also, see my debate with T. F. Green in " 'Teaching, Acting, and Behaving': A Discussion," *Harvard Education Review* 35 (Spring 1965): 192–194, 206–207.

syllables to P—then we may have merely a case of acquired skill in repeating sounds rather than any meaningful sense of the attainment of propositional or verbal knowledge. That is, we might treat such cases as learning or knowing *how* to repeat such words as, "The planets in our solar system travel in elliptical orbits," or, "I pledge allegiance to the flag of the United States of America . . ." and not as learning or knowing *that*.

In any case, it seems plausible that the decision about whether to count parroting as successful teaching *that*, learning *that*, or knowing *that* is open to either a logical or a pedagogical resolution. And the development of such a resolution need not detain us here as long as we can keep such cases intuitively separate from more demanding senses of success in teaching *that*, learning *that*, and knowing *that* which assume that P *understands the proper contextual meanings of the words* in whatever proposition (*x*) we shall use as an example.

But this does not solve all our problems, for, as Scheffler points out, teaching and learning are broader categories than knowing.[17] Truth is a fundamental condition of knowledge. Although I might be taught and, in fact, learn *that* the earth is flat or *that* water boils at 0°C, such propositions obviously do not constitute knowledge about the earth or about the properties of water. "True knowledge" is a redundancy, for we only count as knowledge that which we also count as true. Thus, at least two conditions must hold for the ascription of knowledge to someone. First, the proposition must be true and, second, the person must believe it to be true. Although the ancients may have believed that the earth was flat, we reject the truth of this statement and hence do not count it as part of our store of knowledge today.[18] Yet we would not hesitate to say that someone (in the past or present) can be taught or can learn that the earth is flat. Truth is not a condition of what is taught or learned in the propositional sense.

But, as Scheffler points out[19], meeting the conditions of truth and belief only gives us knowledge in a "weak sense," for we may have no grounds for our true belief other than a lucky guess or an intuitive

17   Israel Scheffler, *The Conditions of Knowledge* (Glenview, Illinois: Scott, Foresman, 1965), see Chapter 1. In this book, Scheffler does a conditions-type analysis on the concept of knowing. In the paragraphs that follow, I first sketch substantively his analysis and then describe the form and strategy used. Material used with permission of the publisher. Copyright © 1965 by Scott, Foresman and Company.

18   Certainly, as Scheffler correctly points out, we count as knowledge the fact *that* the ancients *believed* the earth to be flat, but not the false proposition that the earth *is* flat. Ibid., p. 24.

19   Ibid., pp. 8–9.

leap. Knowing *that* in the "strong sense"[20] demands one more condition, that of having evidence or the right to be sure of what we claim to know. Although teaching and learning can deal with false propositions or with the purveyance and acceptance of true beliefs, it is the evidence condition which forces on us a fuller consideration of both the nature of propositional knowledge and the teaching-learning process.

In essence, the evidence condition requires that we back up our beliefs and provide some grounds or warrant for what we take to be true. It requires that we provide reasons, evidence, or proof for what we assert we know. It is indeed a "strong" sense, for it is not always that we are challenged to back up our statements with some form of proof. But, pedagogically speaking, we generally expect that the young should learn what constitutes adequate evidence, good reasons, or reliable proofs for some beliefs, so that they may be better prepared to acquire knowledge on their own and, in the future, to test their own knowledge claims and those of others.

But what constitutes adequate evidence, proof, or what Ayer[21] aptly calls "the right to be sure"? Scheffler argues that it is not enough just to be in possession of the evidence; one must also have the proper "pattern" in which to place the evidence.[22] One "must *understand* the proof, *see its point.*"[23] To make his point, Scheffler uses the example of a mystery story. Prior to the super sleuth's inevitable announcement of the murderer's identity, all the clues, all the evidence has been woven into the details of the story. The reader *has* the evidence, but it takes the detective to pull it all together in a persuasive pattern before the reader sees that only the butler could have done it. Scheffler goes on to distinguish between *following* a proof (appreciating the force of the detective's "deduction") and *producing* a proof (actually constructing the proper pattern into which to fit the facts).

---

20   Ibid. We may also have our information on good authority, but frequently we wish students to do more than accept facts on authority alone.

21   A. J. Ayer, *The Problem of Knowledge* (Harmondsworth, England: Penguin Books, Ltd., 1956), pp. 31–35. Also see Scheffler's *The Conditions of Knowledge,* the chapter on knowledge and evidence, for a much fuller and more sophisticated treatment of the evidence condition. Up to this point, I have merely echoed the general framework of Scheffler's book to provide the background necessary to answering our question about the successful teaching of knowledge *that.* I strongly recommend Scheffler's book to those who would seek a penetrating, in-depth analysis of this topic.

22   Scheffler, *The Conditions of Knowledge,* pp. 68 ff.

23   Ibid., p. 70.

Notice, however, where this fuller examination of Scheffler's treatment of the evidence condition has taken us. From a concentrated examination of the logical nature of knowing *that,* we have come to talk of knowing *how to* pattern data to constitute a proof. Gathering evidence, supporting our assertions, producing an argument, etc., all seem to involve the use of some complex skills. Thus, knowing *that* in the strong sense seems to involve knowing *how*! Moreover, "seeing the point," "appreciating the force of an argument," or "understanding a proof" all seem to go beyond pro-positional and procedural knowledge altogether to what Scheffler has called "attainments"[24]—attaining a state of appreciation or under-standing, states which "outstrip knowing in range."[25]

In a word, although the distinctions between propositional and procedural knowledge, propensities, and attainments are quite useful in some contexts, there is much to the opposite view that, in the con-text of the down-to-earth business of teaching and learning, we are dealing with an amalgam of the many types of learning, sometimes in very strict conjunction. Therefore, although an analysis of educa-tional concepts may be most helpful to our theoretical understand-ing, we should recognize that an early termination of analysis or a refusal to test analytic results in the concrete may very well produce artificial barriers to practical understanding and application.

Nonetheless, to reach this point we have mixed techniques and types of analysis while using yet another type of analysis, one which focuses on the *conditions* to be met for the proper application of a concept. We have sketched Sheffler's discussion of the **conditions** of knowledge and now should pause to note the form and general strate-gy employed in such **conditions-type analysis. The form the concep-tual question takes is: "Under what conditions or under what circum-stances would it be true to say that** X**?"** (e.g., to say that some-one *knows* something). This is not to seek the general features of what makes a thing (species) a member of a general class; while similar in some respects, its aim is not the same as that of a generic-type analysis. History and math are disciplines under any and all conditions, as are law and medicine professions. There are many things that count as knowledge, but they only count as knowledge

---

24   Ibid., pp. 17-19.

25   Ibid., p. 17. In his own very thorough analysis, only the skeleton of which has been paraphrased here, Scheffler does not seem to recognize this paradox of talking about a "strong" sense of knowing whose elements "outstrip knowing in range." I have tried to treat this paradox more fully in my paper "Analysis and Anomalies in Philosophy of Education," *Proceedings of the Philosophy of Education Society,* 1971.

because of, and only so long as they meet, certain conditions (truth belief, and evidence conditions.) **The point of the general strategy of a conditions-type analysis is to try to identify the necessary and sufficient conditions required to properly apply term x and to test by example cases in which a condition holds, but application of the concept is withheld. This helps locate the need for additional conditions.** Thus, the possibility of claiming to know on the basis of making a lucky guess and being right forces the consideration of an "evidence" condition for knowing in the strong sense. We will see a fuller elaboration of the strategy of conditions-type analysis in the next chapter, as we seek the conditions for giving and receiving a satisfying explanation.

Let us return now to Scheffler's distinction between "following" and "producing" a proof, argument, or pattern of evidence. The importance of this distinction lies in the fact that we would expect one who actually produces a patterning of evidence to see the point or appreciate the force of the pattern created. This is in the very nature of what it means to produce an argument. On the other hand, we have no reason to believe that one who is given a pattern, an explanation, or a proof must thereby *automatically* understand or appreciate its force. These ideas can best be illustrated by putting them into a concrete educational situation, that of teaching history. The traditional western pattern for categorizing historical data is the division into ancient, medieval, and modern periods. Students and historians seem little bothered by the fact that some poor person born in 470 was an *ancient* babe, but soon became a *medieval* child following the fall of Rome in 476. Nor have I ever heard students complain that the modern period (circa 1600–?) is continually expanding until, at some future date, a "modern" will be more ancient in years than any of the "ancient" Greeks or Romans are today.

Suppose, however, that students were offered the opportunity to produce (appreciate and understand) their own temporal patterns of history. I suspect that there would be, instead of a meaningless train of events and dates, an appreciation and understanding of history quite unlike what students now normally take away from most formal history courses. Conceivably, one might look to temporal patterns based on economic phases in Western history (local economies, Mediterranean economy, European economy, colonization and world economy, nation-block economy, and the future) or to a political thematic pattern (tribalisms, cities, city-states, empires, nation-states, world-nation blocks, international government). There are, I suppose, many such patterns which could be produced by teachers or even by students. And they would be followed more easily because they would provide something that has a *point*, something that changes unrelated facts to evidence, isolated events to related and meaningful occurrences, and pieces of a scattered puzzle into a completed picture.

I am not here advocating a method for teaching which all should follow, although I must admit that this approach has considerable appeal to me personally in many teaching contexts. Rather, I would only use this illustration from history to show once again how philosophical analysis can generate practical educational suggestions. It is not so much that analysis leads one naturally to specific programmatic conclusions about educating, but rather that analysis in depth provides a fuller range of clear alternatives for what we desire to do as educators.

Once again, we complete a chapter with many loose strands. We have looked more deeply into the concept of knowledge by examining the various types of knowledge which have been discerned by others out of logical or pedagogical motivations, and we have gone more deeply into the inner logic of knowing *that* by means of an introduction to a conditions-type analysis. Our discussion has not advocated (prescribed) that any one type of knowledge (or, indeed, that only knowledge) is the proper form of subject matter, as did Henderson. Instead, it has provided us with a variety of ideas relevant to what we may choose to be taught and learned. To leave open the choice of what and how to teach is not to abrogate educational responsibility in the realm of educational theory; it is to provide a clearer picture of what the choices are and to invite those who would teach to choose for themselves, on the basis of sound reasons, the methods which —given the logic of the case—now seem most efficient and sensible to them. A good part of what we call teaching does not occur in the classroom itself, but happens in the heads of teachers preparing a lesson or a course, as they lay out their objectives and principles in some order meaningful and sensible to themselves. In taking on this task, theoretical considerations much like those dealt with in this book become quite practical—theory and practice finally can merge.

Learning, explaining, and understanding

4

When all is said and done about educating, it is the actual result of the enterprise which ultimately signals our success or failure. All the high-sounding definitions we mouth, all our arguments about the academic or scientific status of our field, all our logical analyses, the careful selection and organization of subject matter, the development of methods for teaching toward this or that objective—all is for naught unless our students actually learn what we intend they should. We have already seen the vast potential range of "learnings": skills, simple and complex; dispositions, propensities, habits, and attitudes; information, concepts, and theories; appreciations and understandings.

In this chapter, we focus our attention on understanding as a generally recognized desirable outcome of educating. Needless to say, the concept of understanding is a complex one. It will not do merely to say that it is "seeing the point" or "appreciating a pattern," for we must dig deeper than that if some of the means for bringing about understanding are to be illuminated.

We will seek such illumination by way of doing an extended conditions-type analysis of the polymorphous concept, "satisfying explanation."[1] Beyond this, the present chapter will also serve as a

---

1   Ryle identified polymorphous concepts which require a conditions-type analysis in his "Thinking and Language," *Proceedings of the Aristotelian*

vehicle for displaying the analytic techniques demonstrated thus far. Thus, we shall not look for a definition of understanding, but rather for some conditions that must be satisfied if understanding can be said to be achieved by someone. First we will ask a prior question, "Are there various types of understanding or only one?" so that we may distinguish clearly what we would attempt to analyze. Then we will limit the context of our analysis to the seeking of satisfying explanations by someone in search of understanding. This will allow us to consider concrete examples and counterexamples, which will force our ideas into the real world in which education takes place as we perform the conditions-type analysis of satisfying explanation. Finally, we will find that our analysis leads to more questions that need contextual answers, rather than to a definite conclusion that is good for all times and all places.

UNDERSTANDING AND EXPLAINING

In the last chapter, we noted one dominant sense in which we talk of understanding. The discussion of parroting led us to consider the semantic-symbolic sense of understanding, which is used when we are concerned about the comprehension of meanings. Thus one may memorize (learn how to repeat) a phrase or sentence in a foreign language, without knowing what it means. In such a case, we could say the person knows it (knows *how* to say it), but we could also say that the person does not understand what he or she is saying (comprehend its meaning). Certainly this sense of understanding is important, and yet it seems to fall short of what we mean when we say someone understands subatomic theory or constitutional law. The fact that I understand English does not mean that I understand whatever is said to me in English, even though I may know the meanings of the words used. I may know the symbols used in trigonometry, but still may not understand the solutions given for certain trigonometric problems. There is something more to this second sense of understanding beyond understanding the meanings of words

---

Society, supplement 25 (1951): 67–69. Simply put, polymorphous concepts are taken to be concepts whose manifestations assume "many forms." 'Practicing' is such a concept. One might do any number of things while practicing which one might also do when not practicing, like singing. Whereas, for instance, 'walking' or 'crying' do not take "many forms." One can't put feet in front of one another at a certain pace nor drip tears from one's eyes without "walking" or "crying" in the same way one can first *practice* a song and then *sing* it. For an interesting discussion of the nature of polymorphous concepts, see J. O. Urmson, "Polymorphous Concepts," in *Ryle: A Collection of Critical Essays,* ed. by O. P. Wood and G. Pitcher (New York: Doubleday, 1970), pp. 249–266.

or symbols. In the pages that follow, we shall focus our inquiry on this sense.[2]

It may be easier to approach this more profound sense of "understanding" by examining a special context in which this type of understanding is generally sought. We may see a flower bloom in a snowbank in the dead of winter and ask, "How can that be?" Or, we might hear of a machine that reproduces itself and ask, "How does it work?" When genuinely puzzled about something, we seek understanding by asking for an *explanation*. Certainly, we can achieve an understanding of something without asking anyone for an explanation, but when we do ask, we indicate two things. First, we confess our lack of understanding and, second, we indicate our desire to achieve understanding. Granted, such a context is narrow, but at least it provides us with clear cases of individual searches for and achievements of understanding, which we may then attempt to deal with more generally.

It should be obvious that, even if we are given an explanation for something that puzzles us, having such an explanation is no guarantee that we then understand. There are, as it were, two sides to the business of explaining and understanding. The objective structure and content of any explanation may be examined and described, as may be the subjective force it carries or fails to carry for the individual who receives it. On the objective side, there are explanations that are good or bad insofar as they meet an objective standard. They may be evaluated as proper or improper in form without taking into account the psychological state of the individual. There are also good and bad explanations on the subjective side—those that provide an individual with what is necessary to achieve a state of understanding and those that do not—but these demand some consideration of their psychological force. One might suppose that an objectively correct explanation generally would produce understanding, but such is not always the case. We might have Einstein's theory of relativity explained to us in quite proper form, and yet not understand it at all. Although the objective form of an explanation is important to our understanding, those special aspects of the form that are necessary to achieve understanding must be carefully delineated from the objective standards of a good explanation. We shall search, therefore, for those special conditions any explanation must meet if it is to

2   Of course, there is at least one more sense of "understanding"—as in an "understanding person" (sympathetic or empathetic). This, however, is not our prime concern here; we shall not attempt to categorize all the ordinary senses of "understanding."

satisfy an individual to the extent that he or she is willing to say, "Now I understand."[3]

The philosophical literature on explanation has been dominated by the objective concern with the logical structure of explanations; little has been done systematically with what we have described above and which we might call here the subjective dimension of explanation. Philosophers who deal with explanation most frequently act as if there were only one proper objective form of explanation worthy of the name. This is variously called "the covering-law model of explanation," "the deductive model," or, more often, just plain "scientific explanation."

Essentially, the pattern for such an explanation consists of a general law, a set of circumstances "covered" by that law, and a conclusion deduced from these major and minor "premises" which "explains" what was to be explained. An overly simple example should make clear this pattern. Suppose we want to explain the occurrence of ice on a pond. We state the law that water will freeze if the temperature goes below 0°C; then we present the circumstances—the temperature has been below −10°C in the vicinity of the pond; and we reach the conclusion—therefore, ice has formed on the pond. In effect, such explanations say that whenever conditions are such and such, there will be a particular result or concomitant condition: conditions were so, therefore x resulted.

But in our everyday dealings with the world and with others, certainly some explanations are offered and accepted which do not meet these objective criteria of a deductive form of explanation. Not only do some of our ordinary explanations miss the mark by sometimes being incomplete (not having all the relevant laws or circumstances mentioned in them), but they frequently are totally devoid of any deductive pattern, either full or sketchy.

For example, a child might seek an explanation for the white stripe painted down the middle of the road. It would take no great feat of imagination to presume that this could be explained satisfactorily thusly: the stripe is a guideline painted there to provide a visual means by which drivers of motor vehicles can easily keep to their own side of the road in order to avoid hitting others. Now there might be a general law lurking in this explanation somewhere, though I seriously doubt it, or there may be some deductive pattern

---

3   The analysis that follows is based on my paper, "The Subjective Dimension of Explanation," delivered at the annual meeting of the Philosophy of Education Society in 1964 and subsequently published in *The Proceedings of the Philosophy of Education Society* (1965). Permission to use it here has been granted by the Society and publisher.

hidden from view. But I think that the reasonableness of this explanation can better be explained by taking this explanation to be of a *teleological* and not a *scientific* type. It is an attempt to make something understandable to someone in terms of its purpose, not in terms of its relationship to some general law or deductive pattern.

Such nondeductive examples of ordinary explanation could be multiplied and the various forms of explanation classified, as indeed Leonard Swift has done.[4] He points to such types of explanation as the "teleological," the "chronological," the "casual," the "genetic," the "definitional," and the "descriptive," dividing them into "relational" and "nonrelational" forms of explanation. For our purposes, however, the examination of each of these types is not necessary; we need only note that there are some defensible grounds for the assumption that many acceptable forms of explanation exist.

A key consideration with respect to ordinary forms of explanation, as we have already noted, is the question of what gives rise to their occurrence. Quite obviously, explanations are generally given when requested and they usually are requested by someone who is curious or puzzled about something. Thus, a curious wife may ask her husband to explain the lipstick smudge on his collar or a puzzled child may ask why, if mommy is called "doctor," she doesn't have a stethoscope and a little black bag full of pills and lollipops. But not all solicited explanations are requested by someone who lacks an understanding of the thing to be explained. A chemistry teacher, for instance, may ask a student to explain the precipitation of a brownish substance in a test tube not because the teacher doesn't know why the substance precipitated, but because he wants to find out if the student knows why. Though one could legitimately say the instructor in this case asks for an explanation because he is curious about something, it would obviously be inappropriate to assume that he is curious about the phenomenon *for which the explanation is sought*, i.e., the precipitant. Rather, he has what might conveniently be termed a "second-order" curiosity about what his student has learned in his classes. Thus we may distinguish between a first-order solicitation for an explanation (wherein the curiosity is directed toward the thing to be explained) and a second-order solicitation (in which curiosity is directed elsewhere) by noting the motivations of whoever requests the explanation. Making this distinction allows us to limit our treatment to first-order solicited explanations.

Before we leave the notion of solicitation, a further point should be made. Although this distinction separates first-order from second-

---

4   L. F. Swift, "Explanation," in *Language and Concepts in Education,* ed. by Smith and Ennis (Chicago: Rand McNally, 1961), pp. 179–194.

order solicitations for explanations, these should not be taken as mutually exclusive. A father genuinely puzzled about the workings of the stock market and also genuinely curious about what his son has learned as an economics major in college may seek both a first-order and a second-order explanation at the same time. Moreover, both types of solicitation may be satisfied simultaneously by the same explanation although it is conceivable that none or only one of them may be satisfied. This fact, however, should not detract from the essential difference intended by the distinction.

CONDITIONS FOR A SATISFYING EXPLANATION

Given a context in which an individual asks for and receives an explanation of something he or she is curious or puzzled about, we may now reasonably ask what conditions must be met by the explanation offered to make it *acceptable* as an explanation *to the one who asks for it*. In his paper, "Truisms as the Grounds for Historical Explanations,"[5] Michael Scriven provides three prime candidates for our consideration in his discussion of three types of "deficiencies of explanations": inaccuracy, inadequacy, and irrelevancy. In making these distinctions, Scriven is concerned with the form of evidence and the logical grounds necessary to defend an explanation that fails in any of these ways. However, he is not directly involved, as we will be, with an attempt to provide criteria for the acceptability of an explanation by someone with reference to the *psychological satisfaction* of the explanation offered. Nevertheless, if we take Scriven's terms and make them positive, we have three conditions to apply to the *subjective dimension* of explanation, which, even if they prove inadequate to the task, may provide us with some insights into the nature of explanation viewed from the vantage point of the individual receiving a solicited explanation.

Let us begin with the positive notion of relevancy and state, as a first tentative condition, that an explanation, to be a satisfying one, must be of the *type* requested. In a shortened form we may call this the *relevant-type* condition. Its application can be made clear by a very simple, mundane example, which should ring true for all who

---

5   Michael Scriven, "Truisms as the Grounds for Historical Explanations," in *Theories of History*, ed. by Patrick Gardiner (New York: The Free Press, 1959), pp. 443–475. In this paper, Scriven shows much more interest in the context of explanation than do most writers on the subject. I highly recommend the paper to those interested in this topic and herewith acknowledge my debt to Scriven's paper. It provided the germ of many ideas basic to this analysis of the subjective dimension of explanation and related ideas about the phenomenon of understanding.

have attempted to converse with an inquisitive child. It will take little imagination to follow the ensuing dialogue:

"Daddy, why is chocolate ice cream brown?"

"So the man in the ice cream store can tell the difference between chocolate and vanilla when you ask him for one or the other." (teleological-purpose)

"Oh, I know that, but why is chocolate ice cream *brown*?"

"Because chocolate is brown!" (definitional-descriptive)

"But, why *is* it brown?"

"Because light is made up of all the colors of the rainbow, and when it strikes chocolate ice cream, all the other colors are absorbed by the ice cream, allowing only the brown light to be reflected in your eye, and so you see it as brown." (causal)

"Oh, I understand now! . . . Do you suppose all those other colors in the chocolate ice cream are what make it taste so good?"

With your indulgence, I'll end this dialogue here, although its continuation might be more intriguing than the remainder of our analysis. Be that as it may, I hope this example makes clear the need for a relevancy condition in any subjective consideration of explanation. Of course, the order of explanations offered in the above dialogue could have been switched, so that the final satisfying form of explanation might have been the definitional-descriptive or the teleological one.

To hold to the requirement of a relevancy condition, however, poses certain problems. One might conceivably be willing to accept more than one type of explanation and, furthermore, might have little conscious idea of the type or types which would be suitable. But I hope that this fact would not detract from the sense of the requirement. A more serious objection to this condition is that it might not be a sufficient condition. It is conceivable that one could receive an explanation of the relevant type and still not be satisfied with it because of its inaccuracy or for some other reason. Thus one might seek a causal explanation for the ink spilled on the rug, but to be told that little elves of the woodland did it might not be a very satisfactory explanation, even though it is of the relevant type. Hence the relevancy condition obviously cannot stand alone, but is only one important element in describing the nature of an explanation that is psychologically acceptable to someone. Let us then turn to the other conditions suggested by Scriven's analysis in an attempt to locate some of these other important elements.

Scriven describes the inadequacy of an explanation as a failure to "fully [and completely] explain what [it was] supposed to explain . . . ."[6] To frame a positive condition of adequacy, then, we might say that a satisfactory explanation must be psychologically complete. Note that I do not say logically complete. Many times we accept explanations, even of a logical type, which are far from complete as given, but, in receiving them, we ourselves supply the logical connections which make the explanations both psychologically satisfying and logically complete.

For instance, one could ask why the car radiator cracked and receive as a satisfying explanation: "Because water expands when it freezes." This one fact, fitted into all that is already known by the individual (i.e., the car was left out all night, the temperature dropped below 0°C, water was in the radiator, etc.), would *psychologically* complete the gap in understanding by providing the missing link that forges all this information into a relational chain.

In talking about the psychological adequacy or completeness of an explanation, two aspects of completeness must be noted. First, an explanation can be taken to be psychologically incomplete insofar as it has a logical gap or gaps which cannot be or are not filled in by the individual. In the radiator example above, if the reply had been an elaborate noting of all the relevant laws and conditions of the event, omitting only the fact that water expands when it freezes, this logical gap would have made the explanation incomplete and unsatisfactory psychologically. Thus the explanation, as well as the radiator, would have a "hole" in it!

But let us consider a case in which there is no missing element, no logical gap in the explanation offered, and let us further assume that the explanation is of the required type (causal). Imagine a young child seeking an explanation for the cracked radiator; in good "covering law" fashion, an "Uncle Hempel" gives a complete account of all relevant conditions and scientific laws, including such statements as: "Below [0°C], under normal atmospheric pressure, water freezes. Below [4°C], the pressure of a mass of water increases with decreasing temperature if the volume remains constant or decreases; when the water freezes, the pressure again increases . . . as a function of its temperature and volume . . . [etc.]."[7]

There is a good chance that such an explanation would not be satisfying to the child, even though in its fullest presentation there

6   Ibid., p. 446.

7   Carl G. Hempel, "The Function of General Laws in History," in *Theories of History*, ed. by Patrick Gardiner (New York: The Free Press, 1959), p. 346.

would be no logical gaps. Obviously, the inadequacy of this explanation lies in the unfamiliar terminology used. It is inadequate because it fails to complete a *psychological*—not *logical*—connection between what the individual does not understand and what he does understand. This should indicate quite clearly that the adequacy of an explanation viewed in its subjective dimension cannot be assessed on the merits of its logical form alone, but rather must be examined in a specific context with respect to what the individual does and does not already know or understand about the event or phenomenon in question.

But what of the third candidate for condition status: *accuracy*? Certainly, even if viewed from the subjective dimension, one would expect that accuracy is an essential element in making any explanation satisfying. Thus we could demand as our third condition that a satisfactory explanation must be accurate. Scriven aligns accuracy with truth,[8] and I think we all generally assume that truth has a psychological force of its own. Confronted with alternative explanations, both of which are of the relevant type and psychologically adequate, but with one true and the other false, we would expect that the truth would prevail. But we know from historical example that in just such situations people have rejected true explanations and have been satisfied with false ones. Galileo's inquisition is not an isolated historical phenomenon. The opposed explanations of the operations of the solar system, the Ptolemaic and Copernican, had adherents on both sides. I expect we could multiply such examples from the history of science with little trouble.

The fact that some may find a false explanation acceptable should make it quite clear that, from a subjective point of view, we cannot make truth a requirement for *satisfying* explanations. But still, there seems to be something in the accuracy condition which is not contained in the first two conditions. Conceivably a person could receive an explanation of the relevant type which was psychologically adequate for that person in that it had no gaps, was not expressed in unfamiliar language, and was in some way linked with what the individual already understood—and yet be dissatisfied with the explanation. The problem with the Copernican theory for those who rejected it was not that it was of the wrong type or that it had serious logical gaps or used unfamiliar terminology; even in those times an individual could be expected to understand it in terms of familiar experiences. Rather, those who were not satisfied found the theory unsatisfactory because it did not square with their *belief* that

---

8   Scriven, "Truisms as the Grounds for Historical Explanations," p. 446.

the earth was fixed and the sun, moon, and planets revolved around it. For such people, the theory contained a major inaccuracy, though it might be wiser with hindsight to say that it failed to be *consistent* with what they then *believed* to be true.

I submit, therefore, that to be psychologically satisfying, an explanation must not only be psychologically adequate and of the relevant type, but it must also be consistent—or at least compatible—with the *beliefs* the individual holds to be true. Thus, the accuracy requirement could be renamed the compatibility condition, and defined in some such manner as this: "A satisfactory explanation must be subjectively 'accurate' in the sense that it is consistent and is compatible with, or meets the standards imposed by, the beliefs the individual already holds." As much as this statement may seem to commit me to a coherence theory of truth, I would like to point out that what I have, in fact, attempted to do in this reformulation is to separate the notion of truth from the notion of "accuracy," so that this analysis of the subjective dimension of explanation will not be committed to any particular theory of truth.

Although I separate truth from satisfactory explanation in the case of an immediate judgment about an explanation from the subjective point of view, an interesting long-range connection between truth and the compatibility condition should be noted. It would seem to follow from what has been said that the more true beliefs a person holds, the more probable it is that he or she would accept only true explanations. Looked at in this cumulative manner, the third condition has great relevance to education. Though we cannot anticipate what social, economic, political, or natural phenomena may puzzle an individual once that individual has completed a formal education, the reservoir of true beliefs and understandings acquired in that formal education will maximize the probability that the person will not accept false explanations as satisfying, because they will tend to be inconsistent or incompatible with what the person already holds to be true.

There is, however, one major problem concerning the third condition. How, one must ask, while holding to this condition, can one explain the fact that some people do accept explanations like the heliocentric theory, when it is obvious that, prior to the announcement of this theory, they too probably held the view that the earth was the fixed center of the solar system? How, in effect, can true explanations take the place of false ones if truth is not a basic element in the subjective dimension of explanation?

My response must be in the form of what Dray has called a "how-possibly" explanation as distinct from a "why-necessarily" explanation.[9] In other words, I will try to show that the third condition has been stated in such a way as to allow for this to happen, but I cannot say why it happens or go into the contingencies for its happening. The Copernican theory is an ideal case in point. If one believes that the fixed earth is the center of the solar system, then I do not see how one could also hold that the sun is the fixed center. This would be a contradiction, and I am assuming that, to any rational person, such a direct contradiction is not psychologically tolerable. But if the newer explanation is so plausible, so appealing that it causes one to doubt and ultimately reject one's earlier belief, then the newer explanation becomes consistent and compatible with one's present beliefs (which are now devoid of the contradictory belief). At this point, the new explanation becomes acceptable and psychologically satisfactory. However, prior to the rejection of the incompatible belief which was held while receiving and entertaining the heliocentric explanation, it was not—indeed, could not have been—psychologically tolerable, let alone satisfying, because of the presence of the contradiction.

Now, obviously, not all explanations which might be incompatible with certain of our beliefs are contradictions. However, this example is only intended to show that the third condition is consonant with the ordinary phenomenon of changing one's beliefs and accepting new explanations, but no more than that. Given hazier cases, in which certain beliefs would seem rationally to preclude a certain explanation which nonetheless is taken as satisfactory, there may be good reason to reject the third condition or to attempt to modify it in yet some other way if it still seems, as it does to me, to be a necessary ingredient in the consideration of the subjective aspects of the phenomenon of explanation.

We should pause now to sketch the form of a **conditions-type analysis.** Unlike the beginning strategy of a generic-type analysis, in which model cases are identified and essential features are drawn from them, model cases of polymorphous concepts are not so easily located. Therefore, **the first move in a conditions-type analysis is to test an obviously necessary condition of** x **by providing an example which meets that condition, but can easily be made to be an instance of not-x by altering other contextual circumstances.** (For example, although of the right type—causal—the explanation of elves spilling ink was not acceptable.) **This forces either revision or rejection of the condition or leads to the positing of additional conditions for further**

9   W. Dray, *Laws and Explanations in History* (London: Oxford University Press, 1957), pp. 164–169. In effect, I think I can account for how this *may* come about for some people, but I make no claim that it *must* always happen to everyone in just this way whenever a true explanation is offered to replace a false one.

testing by example and counterexample, as we did when we tested
the adequacy condition and generated the compatibility condition
from the Copernican theory example. The purpose of a conditions-
type analysis, then, is to produce the set of necessary and sufficient
conditions for the proper application of a concept to any of its many
and varied instances.[10] A generic-type analysis, on the other hand,
seeks to determine the essential characteristics of the paradigmatic
form of a concept.

LEARNING AND UNDERSTANDING

By means of this analysis, we have examined and modified three
conditions which can be applied to an explanation in order to determine whether or not the explanation will satisfy the individual who
receives it. If the relevant type, adequacy, and accuracy conditions
as defined above have been met by an explanation, I believe we can
then unequivocally say that the explanation offered will satisfy the
individual. But can we now say further that, if these criteria are met,
the individual has achieved *understanding*?

The answer to this question must be "not necessarily," for although the "got-it" feeling of insight, or seeing the point, is psychological in character, the notion of understanding seems to demand
more than a subjective satisfaction with some explanation. Consider,
for example, a man who has just retired for the night. He hears a
glass break and immediately recalls that he left a glass perched pre-
cariously on the window sill above the kitchen sink. Since it is a hot
night, he left the window open, and he reasons that the wind has
blown the curtain against the glass, knocking it off the sill. Satisfied
with this explanation and feeling that he understands what happened, he falls asleep. Waking in the morning, he finds that a burglar
coming through the window had toppled the glass and made off with
the silver.

Thus we speak not only of understanding and not understanding,
but also of *mis*understanding. So our criteria for a satisfying explanation can be met by either a sound or a faulty explanation—or, to
put it differently, can be applied to a case of misunderstanding as
well as to a case of understanding. Although it may be appropriate to
omit the notion of truth from the conditions marking the features of
an explanation that produces a satisfying psychological state in an
individual, the concept of understanding seems to demand more than
satisfaction or seeing the point. It seems that there must be some

---

10   For a further elaboration of this strategy, see the epilogue section,
"Conditions-Type Analysis," pp. 103–107.

justifiable or warranted relationship between what is claimed to be understood and what actually is the case.

Even with this complication, however, we still have a fuller grasp of the notion of understanding than we did before we undertook this analysis of the subjective aspects of explanation. Certainly, the features of compatibility with beliefs already held, lack of logical or psychological gaps, and linkage to what is already known and familiar are key elements in the description of the attained state of understanding. And, what is more, these features suggest points at which the attempt to get someone to understand may break down. These points may be marked on our conceptual map of the teaching-learning situation. If, in any instance of teaching, we choose the destination of understanding *via* explanation, we would have some essential landmarks by which to plan our route. And, if our explanation fails to bring about understanding, we can do more than repeat or rephrase the explanation until we hit upon a satisfactory form by trial and error. Given our analysis, we now have some specific and important clues about what to look for to correct the situation. We can check for the appropriateness of the type of explanation offered, seek to determine if belief consistency is a problem, probe to be assured that there is psychological completeness, and regauge the appropriateness of the level of language of the explanation. Using these checkpoints as a diagnostic tool, we can more intelligently re-route our efforts so as to meet our goal more efficiently and effectively. Moreover, this analysis, with its separation of the logical from the psychological features of explanation and understanding, should make clear that offering a logical and proper explanation of anything is no guarantee that it will be understood. Furthermore, it is no guarantee that the student who says "I see" necessarily understands rather than misunderstands what the teacher has offered. These are but a few of the potential practical applications of the analysis.

This rather lengthy detour through explanation to get at understanding has caused us to neglect a broader view of the general topic of learning. We might justifiably end this chapter, therefore, by summarily treating learning in the context of our total discussion thus far. Although the psychologist may define learning as *a change in behavior*, or the educator as *the acquisition of knowledge*, it should be apparent at this point that such definitions fall far short of the richness of the idea of learning as it is ordinarily used. If we learn about and understand atomic theory, our only change of behavior might be the twinkle of understanding in our eyes. If we learn to be honest, we may acquire no new knowledge at all but merely become disposed to act honestly, whereas before we did not so act, even though we knew that one ought to be honest.

To find out what learning is, one must examine the phenomenon of learning as thoroughly as possible and not expect total enlightenment from any definition or singular approach to learning. There is much work of an empirical sort being done by psychologists in an attempt to lay bare for our illumination the secrets of the mechanics of the learning process. But in these chapters we obviously have not done any empirical work. Rather, we have examined what we already assume about learning as we speak and think about it in our daily lives. Though not empirical, such an exercise still may be valuable and informative, for it forces us to consider ideas we hold but never fully and clearly articulate. This is to say that analysis is not the only or last word to be had about learning, but is merely one of many ways in which we may come to better understand this process so central to the business of educating. To clearly display the crucial subjective factors in understanding for the prospective teacher may prove to be as enlightening or applicable to classroom practice as is the scientific description of behavior-shaping experiments. The complexities of school learning can stand whatever light we might be able to shed on them from whatever quarter, and although we have not dealt fully with learning even from the analytic point of view, we have seen the techniques developed in earlier chapters applied to one complex and most desirable learning outcome: achievement of the state of understanding. In the next chapter, we apply a blend of these techniques and strategies to a further analysis of the concept of teaching.

Teaching revisited

5

We have already dealt with the idea of teaching in a preliminary way while focusing more directly on the concepts of subject matter, knowledge, and satisfying explanations. In this chapter, we use variations on the analytic techniques and strategies introduced thus far to illuminate further the concept of teaching viewed as a dynamic, rational, intentional activity.[1] This chapter is intended to serve two purposes directly in line with the dual focus of this book. By developing a fuller analysis of the concept of teaching, we pursue the substantive analytic goal of clarifying and informing our ways of thinking about teaching. Helping educators to think about teaching in a more sophisticated fashion has been an important substantive contribution of the analytic approach to philosophy of education in recent years. But we also continue our emphasis on technique. While no new strategies or techniques are introduced here, we will observe the analytic thinker at work, not held in check by "recipes" for doing analysis, but set loose to deal with a conceptual problem directly with whatever tools seem appropriate to the task. In this demonstra-

---

1   The analysis in this chapter reflects my further thinking about ideas first explored with Donna Kerr in our article "Locating Teacher Competency: An Action Description of Teaching, *Educational Theory* 24, no. 1 (Winter 1974): 3–16.

tion, I try to show that analytic tools, techniques, and strategies, though they may be described and practiced *simpliciter,* need to be sensitively blended together to be effective in an intelligent application to a conceptual problem. Thus this chapter both analyzes and demonstrates a most artful human activity—*teaching.*

In his article, "Teaching: Act and Enterprise," Paul Komisar differentiates between the use of the term "teaching" as it refers to: (a) an *occupation* one can be said to work at; (b) a general *enterprise* or activity one is engaged in during some specific time period; and (c) a particular *act* of a particular kind.[2] Thus, one might be a teacher (occupation sense), but not be engaged in teaching at the moment because of holidays. Or, one may actually be engaged in the teaching enterprise of trying to get students to learn some math during the fifth period, but not be performing a teaching act at the moment—e.g., opening a widow. Part of Komisar's purpose in differentiating the concept of teaching in this way is to provide a conceptual means for separating teaching acts from nonteaching acts, and, more importantly, to separate a basic sense of teaching from the many kinds of things one might do to get people to learn, like indoctrinating, conditioning, training, etc.[3] Basically, however, it is Komisar's distinction between the enterprise level and the act level of teaching which will be of primary concern to us, for it gets more directly at the kinds of things teachers actually do (teaching acts) when they are teaching (engaged in the general enterprise of trying to get someone to learn something). Obviously, teachers do many different kinds of things when teaching. They question, explain, demonstrate, motivate, listen, make judgments, evaluate, and so on. And it is just these particular kinds of acts that are what teaching is.[4]

---

2   Paul Komisar, "Teaching: Act and Enterprise," *Studies in Philosophy and Education* 6 (1968–69): 168–193.

3   Komisar (p. 178) calls these "cousined activities," related to teaching but not teaching activities *per se.* The purpose of Tom Green's "Topology of the Teaching Concept" is similar: to do a differentiation analysis among what he calls the "family of teaching concepts." Also see Green's book, *The Activities of Teaching* (New York: McGraw-Hill, 1971) and James C. McClellan's more recent treatment of this set of distinctions in his *Philosophy of Education* (Englewood Cliffs, N. J.: Prentice-Hall, 1976).

4   In his *The Activities of Teaching,* Green distinguishes between acts he calls "logical and strategic acts of teaching" and "institutional acts" (taking attendance, keeping reports, etc.). Komisar distinguishes between "learning-donor," "learning-enhancing," and "intellectual acts" of teaching. These distinctions are used to group different kinds of acts by noting the function they are intended to perform within the teaching enterprise. We will return to such distinctions later when we sketch a differentiation-type analysis of teaching acts.

Teaching is not some peculiar act different and separate from other kinds of acts. Teaching is what teachers do while engaged in the general enterprise of trying to get people to learn.

Perhaps our vehicle formula, "S teaches P x so that y," will provide yet another way to display these preliminary conceptual points about teaching and lead us to the focal point of our own analysis of teaching. If we take the whole formula to be a description of the enterprise level of teaching, wherein someone is trying to get someone else to learn something, then the word "teaches" would become the place holder for the multiple kinds of acts individuals might perform as teachers. Thus we could denote by x or y or both what learning the teaching act was aimed at and substitute for the general term "teaching" any number of specific acts performed by a teacher trying to bring that learning about. For example, in trying to get P to learn that Columbus discovered America, so that P may begin to get a grasp of his heritage, S could do any number of things. S might didactically describe Columbus's voyage or require P to read about Columbus or show P a film depicting the voyage. Any one of these or any number of such acts would count as teaching acts, because, unlike raising a window, they are clearly directed at trying to bring about learning.

But if, as suggested, "teaches" in our formula stands in place of any teaching act, and if S were to ask P who discovered America so that S could find out if P *had* learned x, then we would seem to have an example of a teaching act that does not have the transparent intent of *producing* learning, but rather is an act aimed at *evaluating* whether learning has occurred. Let us consider another example of an ordinary teaching act that seems not to be directly aimed at producing learning. Imagine a teacher demonstrating the proof of a theorem. While this activity could be directed at getting students to learn the proof, it takes little imagination to suppose this to be a teaching act directed only at getting students to follow the proof, just as one might try to get anyone to follow (not learn) an argument.

Such possibilities suggest that teaching acts may not necessarily be directly aimed at bringing about learning and lead Komisar to argue more broadly that, while learning is the goal of the teaching enterprise, it logically cannot be the goal of each teaching act.[5] Because of the variety of teaching acts possible, Komisar argues that such acts can have no single purpose, but must vary widely as to goals—for example, getting students to follow an argument, solve a problem, understand relations, gain some perspective, answer ques-

5   Komisar, "Teaching: Act and Enterprise," p. 197.

tions, etc. He states, "It is not [directly] some kind of learning, but some form of awareness which is the intended upshot in the [intellectual] teaching acts under discussion."[6]

It would seem that we have good reason, therefore, to look more closely at the concept of teaching as a goal-directed activity if we are to make sense of these claims and of the relation between teaching acts and enterprises.

TEACHING: ACT AND ENTERPRISE

Recall that we followed Sheffler's lead in taking teaching to be an intentional activity generally aimed at trying to get someone to learn something. At the "enterprise level," this would indeed seem to be the mark which distinguishes teaching enterprises from nonteaching enterprises: the same acts might be performed, but with a different general purpose or goal in mind. Thus, a used-car salesman might perform certain kinds of teachinglike acts— questioning, explaining, demonstrating, motivating— but with the intent of selling cars, not of getting people to learn about cars. It is the general intent of these acts, seen in their relation to the enterprise, and not always their immediate goal or characteristics which allow us to mark them as selling acts rather than as teaching acts or vice versa. Therefore, we need a clearer understanding of this relation between teaching acts and the teaching enterprise if we are to make conceptual sense of what it is teachers are doing when they teach.

First we should note that there is an important difference between engaging in an enterprise and performing an act. In a way, such enterprises are a set of acts. We have already seen that during the duration of one's engagement in the teaching enterprise one might perform non–enterprise-related acts like opening a window. But more important, it should be recognized that a single act doth not an enterprise make. Ordinarily, except in rare, single-act enterprises, the teaching enterprise is made up of a set of related acts whose general intent is to produce learning. Thus, each teaching act has two dimensions— its own internal structure of acting to some immediate purpose via some particular form of activity (questioning, demonstrating, motivating, etc.) and its external dimension, i.e., its relation to the other acts taken as parts of the enterprise viewed as a whole.

Thus we are forced conceptually to recognize the obvious. Teaching is not performing a single act, or even a series of single acts, each

---

6   Ibid., p. 184.

aimed at bringing about learning. Rather, teaching is a dynamic, continuous performance of many related acts designed to provide the conditions for bringing about various sorts of learning. But this is to put the obvious conclusion before the cumbersome analytic horse. We must embark on an analysis of teaching as a dynamic, rational, intentional set of activities to justify these conceptual claims.

Before pressing on, it might be useful to review exactly why this analysis is called for. We are saying that teaching ordinarily refers to the many different acts a teacher performs with the general intent of bringing about learning. But we admit that some acts performed by teachers while teaching are not teaching acts (opening windows), on the grounds that they are not related to the general enterprise. Other acts are directly aimed at the general goal of the enterprise of bringing about learning and, hence, clearly are teaching acts (telling students that Columbus discovered America or that the chemical symbol for water is H_2O with the intent that they learn these things). But some acts not directly aimed at producing learning still seem to be more directly related to the enterprise than does opening windows. Such an act might be demonstrating a theorem's proof and trying to get the students to follow it (not learn it) or asking questions of a student not in order to get him to learn the answer, but only to see if he has already learned it. Thus, in our analysis, it would seem that we need to find a way to include as teaching acts some, but not all, acts whose goal is *not* learning.

A prior conceptual question is in order here regarding the nature of any enterprise, be it teaching, farming, selling cars, or playing basketball. Such enterprises are clearly sets of activities rationally performed in the pursuit of some goal. We will call them "rational-intentional" enterprises to indicate that they are not automatic or purely mechanical kinds of activities—like assembly-line behavior, for example—but require foresight, intelligence, flexibility, and mindful behavior to achieve the desired goal or goals of each set of activities.

For instance, one could describe the general enterprise of farming in terms of a sequence of serial activities, each activity a prerequisite to the next. The farmer cultivates the soil, plants the seed, fertilizes and waters the fields, controls for disease and insects while the crop grows, and, when the plants bear fruit, harvests the fields. Such a description clearly represents the general and common form of engaging in a sequential rational-intentional set of activities. I am sure that many activities of teachers, from the general planning of courses to the way in which they develop ideas in a lecture or structure a laboratory exercise, could be seen to have the requisite features of this means-ends-continuum view of a sequential intentional enterprise.

There is, however, another general form of rational-intentional activity which also is clearly reflected in the activities of farming and teaching, but is different from the sequential-intentional. Even though it lacks the idea of set sequence leading to a goal, it is still goal oriented and is still an intelligent-rational activity on the part of the actor. Consider the game of basketball and think for a moment about the basketball player. His general enterprise is intentional and can be characterized in simple terms by his trying to accomplish two things: first, to score as many points against his opponent as possible; second, to keep his opponent from scoring points against him. Now there is no neat sequence of pass the ball, dribble the ball, shoot the ball that leads to the scoring of a goal. The scoring sequence is not invariable; there are many unique configurations of players and play that can never be anticipated, even though some of what goes on may be seen to follow the sequence dictated by routine plays. The important thing to recognize here is that the basketball player does have a clear set of intentions and is making judgments and choices and paying attention to what he is doing and what is happening around him as he decides to pass the ball, dribble the ball, shoot, jump for the rebound, run back to his own court to defend, and so on. We should all recognize that there are times when the teaching enterprise comes closer to this basketball player's flexible, purposive action than it does to the sequential model represented by the farming example.

Moreover, if we look at these two ways of describing rational-intentional human activities, it quickly should be apparent that it is much easier to outline the elements of a sequential performance, where one step is dependent on the other to lead to the result desired, than it is to describe the unpredictable, flexible, serial performance of an intelligent "inter-actor." Nevertheless, noting this difficulty does not relieve us of the task of trying to solve the sticky conceptual problem of describing this dimension of the teaching enterprise. And so, we move on.

TEACHING AS FLEXIBLE, INTELLIGENT ACTION

So as not to leave the wrong impression about farmers, let us return to that example, recognizing that good farming demands just what good basketball playing demands—flexible and intelligent responses to changing contextual variables, even within the constraints of a generally sequential enterprise. An intelligent farmer doesn't water the crops if it has been raining every day. Like the basketball player and the teacher, the farmer acts with one eye on goals and the other on the relevant facts of the immediate situation. In fact, it is these two features—general goals and situational factors—which provide us with what is needed to begin to describe the important conceptual dimensions of the teaching enterprise. We have already seen that what distinguishes a teaching enterprise from a farming or selling enterprise is the general goal of the teaching enterprise—trying to get someone to learn something. But trying to get someone to learn something can only be done in a concrete context, in which certain dimensions of the situation will be relevant to the determination of just what sorts of things count as trying to do *this* and not something else. Watering rain-soaked fields does not count as trying to get crops to grow; lecturing on fetching does not count as trying to teach my dog a new trick. What we are saying, then, is that the acts performed are context dependent in two senses. First, they must be done with the ultimate enterprise goal in mind and, second, they must be appropriate not just to the general goal, but also to the immediate situation at hand. These two factors, the general goal and specific situation, describe the paramenters of any teaching enterprise. Each single act undertaken while engaged in the enterprise, if it is to be undertaken as an intelligent teaching act, must be chosen with these factors in mind and judged to be reasonably related to both.

But while it makes sense to speak of trying to get someone to learn something, it makes little sense to speak of operating with such a general goal in any *specific* situation. Once we recognize that specifying the situation is the key to determining if any specific act is a teaching act within some particular enterprise, it should be clear that we commonly act in some specific teaching enterprise with some specifiable learning goal or goals in mind. As we have already pointed out, one must be trying to get someone to learn *something*. Thus, the math teacher is after mathematical learning and not just learning in general and, further, is usually aiming at algebraic or geometric or some other more specifiable subset of general mathematical learnings. Of course, the math teacher might also be interested in students learning to be courteous or to be good citizens, or whatever. Multiple general learning goals may be operative in any teaching enterprise. In fact, it would seem to be more often the case than not that teachers engaged in a teaching enterprise bring with them a number of general learning goals, some of which they specified in advance in their notes, plans, or minds and others which pervade most all of their teaching and are seized on as relevant and worth pursuing when the situation is propitious.

Having a variety of goals and dealing with a variety of situational factors, some of which are predictable in advance and some of which are not, does not make for chaos; rather, it provides a rich mix which nurtures intelligent, flexible, and reasonable choice, judgment, and action on the part of teachers. Viewed in this way, teaching is not the mechanical following of someone else's plans or even the slavish adherance to one's own. It is the adaptive, intelligent merger of one's goals with the possibilities and limits of the concrete situation.

Let us turn now to the specific acts which, together, constitute the enterprise as a whole. We have already noted that discrete acts by teachers may be of many sorts—questioning, demonstrating, drilling, motivating, explaining, disciplining, etc.—each having its own end, but also related in some way to an end beyond itself, i.e., to some general learning goal. Komisar has argued that certain of these acts cannot be directly aimed at learning, but I would modify his position and argue that each and every teaching act need not be aimed directly at bringing about learning, although any particular act might be. Thus, there are two ways to view the relation of teaching acts to general learning goals. Some acts may be directed at securing a bit of learning that is "analytic"[7] to the general learning goal and some may be directed at achieving ends which may serve as *vehicles* for getting to a general learning goal (but which are not themselves bits of the general learning aimed at). Thus a teacher might drill pupils in addition, subtraction, and multiplication so that students will learn simple number facts, each of these bits of learning contributing to what it means to know number facts. Or, a teacher might elegantly describe a personal experience he has had so that students will be put in a receptive frame of mind to read some poetry. It is easy to see that any teacher action directly aimed at bringing about the learning of something is a teaching act, but other acts, like describing a personal experience or even opening a window, become teaching acts only if they relate to some specific teaching-learning goal, however indirectly. While each individual teaching act must have a goal, that goal need not be learning *per se*. There are many ways to set the stage for learning, some more direct than others.

Moreover, there is still another way to view the potential variety of individual teaching acts and the choices and judgments teachers make as they act in this way or that while engaging in the teaching enterprise. Imagine two teachers with the same immediate teaching goal, that of stimulating interest in emotive poetry by reference to

---

7   This means that it is logically a part of what the goal is. This point is made in the Kerr-Soltis article, "Locating Teacher Competency: An Action Description of Teaching," p. 11.

personal experience. One teacher could try to spark student interest in the poetry by describing his own personal experiences and the other by asking the students to write paragraphs descri_ _ng their own experiences. Having the same immediate goa'_ doe_ not mean having to act in the same way. There are, as we have often been told, many ways to skin a cat. Teachers develop and depend on a variety of tactics and techniques to achieve similar goals. In trying to get some-one to learn number facts, for instance, one could do several things, from directing singsong rote drills to asking each student to collect such facts from daily experience and record them in an arithmetic journal. These examples should make it clear that there are two related elements in all teaching acts, whether directed at learning or not[8]: the immediate *goal* and the appropriate *tactic*. Both require choice and judgment on the part of the teacher, with intelligent reference made to one's general learning goals and the immediate situational factors.[9]

While we have been paying attention to discrete elements in the teaching-act–enterprise relationship, I hope it has been clear that we have been trying to provide a conceptual picture of teaching which is not static and partitioned, but sufficiently dynamic and interrelated to describe teaching in its richer complexity. There is a fluidity and flexibility governed by sensitivity and rationality in teaching which is hard to capture in any analytic treatment, but which is essential to a full description of the enterprise. Our analysis has aimed at display-ing these basic characteristics.

TEACHING DIFFERENTIATED

Our consideration of teaching act and enterprise also has brought us to the point where a differentiation-type analysis of what teachers do when they teach is now possible. We have seen that, while engaged in a teaching enterprise, a teacher may act in many ways. Given our analysis above, let us see if we now can classify types of teaching acts

---

8   In the Kerr-Soltis paper, we accounted for non–learning-directed acts by including them in "complex tactics."

9   Nell Noddings, in her paper, "Teacher Competency: An Extension of the Kerr-Soltis Model," *Educational Theory* 24, no. 3 (Summer 1974): 284-290, argues that teacher judgments may be based on certain other factors, such as a teacher's knowledge and beliefs. I agree with her and would only add that the Kerr-Soltis paper also included the idea of a teacher needing a repertoire of skills and specialized techniques to draw on as well. Thus, we identified a third factor present in all teaching acts—the act of implementing one's choices of tactics and goals. I recommend both papers as good illustrations of analytic technique and critique of a more advanced sort than provided in this introductory text.

in some pedagogically meaningful way. First we should note that nonteaching acts are possible in the midst of any teaching enterprise, but they are distinguished by not having any relation to the teacher's general learning goals. They should be kept separate from non-learning-goal teaching acts, as we have frequently done in our discussions above. Not so easy to set aside, however, are boarderline cases of what Green has called "institutional maintenance acts."[10] Looking out the window is clearly different from taking attendance or dismissing classes on time. These latter acts, while non-learning-directed acts, still do not fall into the same category as demonstrating proofs or stimulating student interest in poetry. But because they have more of a relation to the teacher role as institutional functionary, we might be able to distinguish them by noting their relation to teaching as occupation. At this time, however, so that we might move on to carve out some more useful distinctions among teaching acts themselves, we will merely note in passing the possibility of distinguishing among nonteaching acts.

We have already indicated that teaching acts may be of either a direct learning-goal type or a vehicle type. But we also can further differentiate between them with respect to their primary orientation— whether they are directed toward the *assessment* of situational factors or toward the *manipulation* of situational factors conducive to the achievement of learning goals. Thus, diagnostic or evaluative acts—like asking questions of students to see if they are advanced enough in math to understand chemical equations or asking questions to see if students have learned the vocabulary words of the day—clearly seem to be aimed directly at assessing situational factors. On the other hand, such acts as questioning students about their personal experiences or asking them to read about Columbus's voyage are more directly concerned with bringing about conditions that are likely to lead to the successful achievement of learning goals. While teachers may perform many different types of teaching acts, we should note that teachers achieve their general enterprise goal only as students come to learn. And, while there is much that the intelligent and skillful teacher can do to provide situations conducive to learning, the success of teaching depends as much on good "studenting" as it does on good teaching. Student acts may require as full an analysis as that given to teaching acts, but that raises a whole other set of questions which cannot be pursued here.

So we have come full circle. Once again our extended discussion of teaching has taken us back to learning and to many of the other concepts we have dealt with in this book on education. In this

---

10   T.F. Green, *The Activities of Teaching* (New York: McGraw-Hill, 1971).

chapter, in which we extended our analytic treatment of teaching as an intelligent and flexible activity, I have likewise tried to use the strategies and techniques described in this book in an intelligent and flexible fashion. Like teaching, the art of analysis cannot be learned as a set of mechanically applied skills or techniques. The use of any techniques need to be intelligently guided by one's own purposes and the relevant situational factors. Analysis should serve as an instrument for increasing understanding and for suggesting practical applications.

So saying, it might be fitting to end this chapter with a few words about the potential relevance I see for this analysis of teaching to research, training, and curriculum considerations in teacher education. I personally believe that an analysis of teaching as act and enterprise can serve as a valuable heuristic conceptualization of teaching for researchers to use in designing research on teaching. Even though complex and somewhat amorphous, this conceptualization would direct educational research toward a most important human dimension of teaching.[11] Empirically one might look for naturalistic descriptions of complex teaching acts serially related or designed in some strategy form or pattern to achieve certain kinds of general learning goals. Or, one might invent ways to measure intelligence-in-action or rational response to relevant situational factors. Any number of useful research problems could come out of such a conceptualization.

Similarly, given a language with which to locate and talk about various types of teaching acts and their relation to a particular teaching enterprise or episode, one could help prospective and practicing teachers see the need to make reasonable judgments about what to do and how to do it in light of situational factors, immediate and general goals, and relevant tactics. A category system helps people see what otherwise is hard to pick out. The system sketched here also would underscore the need for teachers to think about what they are doing before, during, and after doing it, and would provide them with tools for doing that thinking flexibly and effectively.

And, finally, the analysis allows us to show how the many components of a standard teacher-education curriculum can directly enter into an individual's acts as a teacher in the classroom; so often, such theoretical studies seem remote from practice. Clearly, it would be reasonable to assume that a person draws his or her general and

---

11   This is not to imply that this avenue of approach to research on teaching has been overlooked or ignored. The pioneering work of such researchers as A. Bellack, H. Taba, N. Gage, and B. O. Smith and their many colleagues and followers has been exemplary in this regard.

more immediate teaching-learning goals from an in-depth knowledge of the subject-matter field and his or her beliefs about its value and use. Intelligent teacher choices are also dependent on an extensive knowledge of curricular options and of alternative approaches to teaching and learning. One's general goals also reflect one's view of the good life, the good society, and the good world, as it might be drawn from philosophical and historical perspectives. To be able to intelligently assess the educational situation, one needs the best diagnostic and evaluative tools available. These can be provided by the social and behavioral sciences, which also can substantively inform one's understanding and appreciation of a multitude of relevant situational factors. To be sensitive to human concerns requires breadth in humane learning. And finally, to be able to choose and use effective tactics and techniques depends on one's knowledge and training in specific methods of teaching. In short, to educate, one must be broadly educated, so as to be prepared to act in an intelligent and flexible manner.

Analysis:
its limits and uses

6

With our analytic investigations of such central educational concepts
as subject matter, knowing, teaching, learning, and understanding
behind us, the time has come to put "philosophical analysis" itself
into a broader perspective. We might have done much more, by way
of deeper and fuller analysis, with the concepts already discussed.
Moreover, there are many other concepts and phenomena relevant to
the enterprise of educating which might also have legitimately
claimed our attention in these pages, "studenting" for example.
But by singling out these few basic concepts and by simplifying
and demonstrating a few of the techniques currently employed by
analytic philosophers of education, I have tried to help the reader
develop a feeling for what philosophical analysis is and does, even
though we have not taken the "whole watch" apart or even put much
of it back together again. Yet I hope that the intent of these pages
to introduce and acquaint the reader with the philosophical analysis
of educational concepts has been effected and that our sketchy examination of some of the component concepts of education has also
provided a richer and more sophisticated view of the complex logic
and assumptions which stand behind many of our ordinary ideas
about educating.

TRADITIONAL PHILOSOPHY AND ANALYSIS

There are ways other than analysis to philosophize about education, and in this chapter we shall look at some of them, so that we may better view and judge the limits and uses of analysis.[1] Most obviously missing from these pages has been any attempt to provide a comprehensive and systematic view of reality, of the total workings of the universe, of our place therein, and of the meaning of life inself. This sort of philosophizing is recognized by many to be the traditional and dominant role of the philosopher and, as such, has been seriously pursued by some of the greatest minds in western history. This compelling search for "the meaning of it all" has been and still is a task taken on by many philosophers. Often, such original thinkers as Plato and Dewey included a detailed picture of education in their comprehensive philosophies. But more frequently, we do not find such elaborations on education offered by major philosophers themselves. Therefore, philosophers of education have set themselves to the task of adopting the world view of such philosophers or some school of philosophy and deriving from that view a consistent and adequate philosophy of education. Thus we frequently have offered to us a philosophy of education, including a full-blown educational theory and a correlative discussion of the practices of educating, framed in the larger context of a comprehensive philosophical system.

Some analytic philosophers have been critical of this traditional way of going about educational philosophizing. For example, D. J. O'Connor, bluntly states that "the traditional philosophers promised more than they were able to deliver and their claims to interpret the universe on a grand scale must be rejected for the same reasons that the claims of alchemists, astrologers, or magicians are now rejected . . . [because their results are not] publicly testable, reliable, and coherent with the rest of public knowledge."[2]

In my estimation, such a reaction is both too presumptuous and too harsh. There is nothing inherent in the analytic approach to philosophizing about educational ideas and phenomena which

---

1   The discussion that follows concerning the various perspectives philosophers of education provide is a distillation of some of the ideas I presented in my article, "Philosophy of Education: A Fourth Dimension," *Teachers College Record* 67 (April 1966): 524–531.

2   D. J. O'Connor, *Introduction to the Philosophy of Education* (London: Routledge & Kegan Paul Ltd., 1957), p. 17. Reprinted by permission.

necessarily rules out other types of philosophizing. To argue and demonstrate the difference between two tasks is not at all to show that one is right and the other wrong. The traditional search for a total philosophical context and understanding of human life in its broadest terms has been a recurrent theme throughout the intellectual history of man; as such, it cannot be rejected out of hand. The question of the "truth" of some world view can be kept separate from the question of its value as a sensible and coherent pattern for guiding the process of educating. Philosophizing in this broad sense may be done well or poorly, but its potential to provide perspective, meaning, and inspiration for those who educate cannot be denied.

Indeed, analysis and world-view making may work in tandem. The techniques of analysis may be used to clarify and make more precise and intelligible the broad and comprehensive concepts of synoptic philosophical systems. We have already seen how the techniques of analysis can force abstract and vague ideas into concrete and more meaningful contexts. Utilizing such techniques, we may sometimes find that a concept is empty or merely honorific, much as we did in our examination of the concept of a discipline. Such a finding can free us from literally senseless debates. In the case of our analysis of the concept of a discipline, for instance, we might well have moved beyond the time-consuming debates over the academic status of education as a field of study to direct our attention and energies to the very heart of the matter: the effectiveness of the field of study itself, as determined by the soundness of its various claims to knowledge and its successes or failures in dealing with the matters in its domain.

Or, utilizing the techniques of analysis on broad and comprehensive concepts, we might find that a certain systemic ambiguity is more desirable than an artificial precision, much as we did in our examination of the concept of subject matter. Becoming more fully aware of the various types of referents for the term "subject matter," we were able to think more directly and efficiently about the many potential objectives for teaching and learning. And we saw that, by utilizing other analytic techniques to pin down general ideas, we might even succeed in determining a set of clear conditions which must be met if a particular concept is to be strictly applicable in any particular context. This was the case with respect to our analysis of the subjective dimension of explanation and the concept of understanding. Finally, developing a conceptual map of teaching act and enterprise provided us with a clearer view into that complex human activity. In these ways, the techniques of analysis may be used effectively in the domain of traditional philosophy of education without necessarily being negative or destructive.

If we could liken the use of analysis to the use of a microscope (and some also use this instrument well or poorly), then we might also liken the traditional philosophical world-view building to the astronomer's use of the telescope in charting the universe. The instruments are designed for different tasks, and so we should expect different results from their respective uses. But the fruitful use of one does not preclude or deny the validity of the use of the other; nor does it cancel the possibility that they may be used in conjunction or in some other complementary way. Thus I would argue that, although there are certain limits to philosophical analysis, these limits are not as narrow and circumscribed as some contemporary philosophers of education believe. In a word, these two approaches are not necessarily antithetical and can complement each other in the unending philosophical attempt to better conceptualize and understand the complex process of education from every available vantage point.

Traditionally philosophers have been concerned with more than providing a broad view of the way the world *is;* they also have directed their attention to a formulation of what *ought* to be, of what is good, right, and proper. Thus another major task taken on by the philosophers of education has been to deal with the value dimensions of education. Once again, it should be obvious that in this introduction to the analysis of educational concepts, we generally have avoided questions of value and, in fact, have attempted to act neutrally with respect to commitments to specific value positions. I have already indicated that this is not to deny the close connection between education and value judgments, for I do agree with Peters that educating always involves questions of value in a very important way. But while this is so, one of the strengths of the neutral stance of analysis is its potential to provide a methodological means to hold our own values at bay while we search into the logical features of educational ideas. In this way, the techniques employed by the analytic philosopher resemble the value-neutral techniques of the social scientist, who attempts thereby to control an inquiry and produce results which are objective in the sense that others who may hold different values still may agree with the results obtained.

Yet there is an important limit to analysis here, for we *must* make decisions of value in educating and pure neutrality is neither desirable nor possible. Value decisions are made every day in the practical and theoretical worlds of educating, and it is the normative philosopher who comes to this problem area uniquely armed with a scholarly knowledge of ethical systems and a disciplined mode of inquiry for dealing with problems of value. In this sphere of educational decision and program making, neutrality is impossible. Thus, the normative philosopher who attempts to provide to the best of his

or her ability a reasonable and well-grounded consideration of what
ought to be done in education fills an important gap beyond the
limits of analysis. Once again, this task may be performed well or
poorly, and we must carefully judge the validity of the grounds and
reasons offered for certain value positions advocated by such philosophers. But in the last analysis, there is no denying the need for intelligent inquiries and reasonable proposals in the realm of educational
values.[3]

ANALYTIC PHILOSOPHY AND THE VALUE DOMAIN

Although I have tried throughout this work and especially in this
chapter to make clear the limits of the analytic approach in the realm
of values, I fear I may have given the impression that analytic
philosophers refrain altogether from dealing in any way with ethics
or questions of value. This is hardly the case,[4] and I would like to take
this opportunity to show by means of an extended example one of the
ways in which analytic techniques may be used to bring more clarity
to educational problems in the realm of values.

We have already conceded that, in a most important sense, the
very idea of educating implies that something of value is being
passed on or learned. Furthermore, we have claimed that value decisions and judgments are made every day in education. However, we
have not paid any attention to another phenomenon which seems to
be equally pervasive in the value dimension of education—the real
and lively areas of disagreement between educators over certain
values or educational programs. Thus, even though we might all
agree that something of value must be passed on to the younger
generation, the crucial question remains: Just *what* of value should

---

3   I should caution the reader not to construct neat pigeonholes to
categorize philosophers on the basis of what I have said above about the
various tasks taken on by philosophers of education. It is not unusual to
find a philosopher whose work involves, at one and the same time, an
analysis of key concepts, a building of a metaphysical view of reality, and
the construction of an ethic or value system. For a fuller elaboration of this
point, see my paper, "Philosophy of Education: A Fourth Dimension,"
Teachers College Record 67 (April 1966): 527–528.

4   Analytic philosophers such as A. J. Ayer, C. L. Stevenson, R. M.
Hare, and others have had a great impact on modern philosophical treat-
ments of ethics, but this is too long a story to be dealt with in detail here.
John Wilson has also contributed significantly and directly to ideas about
the curriculum and teaching of moral education. Another important analytic treatment of values and education is *Ethics and Education* by R. S.
Peters (London: George Allen & Unwin Ltd., 1966). See the "Bibliography"
section of this text for additional pertinent analytic references.

be passed on?[5] Sometimes such questions are phrased in the broad terms of aims and objectives for schooling, and we have already given some analytic consideration to this phenomenon. But disagreements also arise on a more manageable level of concreteness—for example, concerning additions to or deletions from a school curriculum. Thus, more down-to-earth disagreement over values is a fact of daily educational life and, as such, provides a fertile ground for analysis.

One philosopher, C. L. Stevenson, is well known for his perceptive analysis of the phenomenon of disagreements over values.[6] A brief exposition of his ideas as they might be applied to a concrete example from education demonstrates first, that the techniques of analysis can be used in the area of value considerations, and, second, that while these techniques may not solve the substantive problems of specific disagreements, they enable us to more clearly discern important features involved in many of the debates over educational values.

Basically, Stevenson provides us with a distinction between what he calls "disagreements in belief" and "disagreements in attitude," arguing that there is not a logical connection between them, but that there is a psychological one.[7] He suggests that in many of our disagreements over some value we really are disagreeing over two things, or on two different levels and not just one. One form of disagreement is located in the emotive or preferential domain of personal taste (our attitudes or feelings, positive or negative, about something). To illustrate, let us imagine ourselves at a high-school curriculum meeting at which the following happens: One teacher, recalling years of suffering as a student in required Latin courses, feels that there is no need to continue to inflict such torture on all present and future college-bound youth merely because of tradition, and so he proposes that Latin be dropped from the college-preparatory curriculum. Hardly believing his ears, the Latin teacher, with a full life invested in Latin and a love for his subject, strongly objects. If we were to go no further, but merely let these two square off toe to toe, we would probably hear:

---

5   In my paper, "Men, Machines, and Morality," in *The Proceedings of the Philosophy of Education Society*, 1968, pp. 15–19, and reprinted in Chazan and Soltis, eds., *Moral Education* (New York: TC Press, 1974), I argue that this question is at the heart of any moral education program via an analysis of the prior question: What makes a rule a moral rule?

6   C. L. Stevenson, "The Scientist's Role and the Aims of Education," *Harvard Educational Review* 24 (1954): 231–238. Also see "The Nature of Ethical Disagreements," *Sigma* 1–2, nos. 8–9 (1947–48).

7   Ibid.

> "Latin is exciting!"
> "No, Latin is dull!"
> "Latin is alive and beautiful!"
> "No, Latin is dead and ugly!"

Obviously, we are hearing a disagreement centered on the teachers' differing *attitudes* toward Latin.

Although I suspect that some of our educational debates over values never really get beyond this clash of attitudes and, hence, in principle are unresolvable, some people do proceed from such bare statements of their preferences or assumed values and demand good reasons or evidence from one another. Thus we get into the area designated by Stevenson as disagreements in *belief.* To show what is involved here, let's continue our imaginary (and obviously carica-tured) debate over the need for Latin in the high-school curriculum.

> "But," says our Latin teacher, "the study of Latin increases English vocabulary and produces better writers of English prose."

> "Does it really? Can you prove that?" (Notice here we get a demand for proof, while no demands for evidence of one's like or dislike of Latin seemed necessary earlier.)

> "Yes, I've taught Latin for years and have seen my students develop their English vocabulary and also receive excellent grades in English composition after taking Latin."

> "But," says the protagonist, "I just happen to have here in my briefcase a set of psychological studies which show that there is no significant advance in vocabulary for those who study Latin over those who do not, and similarly, that there is no significant difference between the writing skill of any group which studies Latin and that of a group which does not."

Our debate now may move in many different directions. The Latin teacher may deny the validity of the evidence and/or produce counterevidence of his own. He may accept the evidence and yet make new claims for the value of Latin. These claims may also be countered by further evidence, until he reaches a point where all of his *beliefs* about the efficacy of Latin have been demolished by the evidence presented and he is led to change his mind about requiring Latin for all. Of course, it is equally possible that, even though his beliefs have been shown to be false, he will not give in, but will merely retreat to his attitude about the value of Latin and refuse to change his mind about the need for all to take it.

In short—and this is Stevenson's point with respect to a psychological (and not a necessary and logical) connection between attitudes and beliefs—a change in belief *may* have sufficient psychological force also to bring about a change in attitude, but such is not necessarily always the case. While this makes it clear that we may fail to settle a disagreement over values no matter what evidence we offer for our position, what seems most important here is the realization that there is a very pertinent relationship between the truth and falsity of one's beliefs and the value positions one adopts. Stevenson's analysis of disagreements thus provides us with a fuller and clearer picture of the nature of disagreements over values. Although it may not provide a surefire way to resolve questions of value, it does throw needed light on some important components of educational debates over values.[8]

As the above discussion illustrates, the neutral stance of the analytic philosopher need not deter him or her entirely from using analytic techniques in the realm of values, even though there is a very important sense in which normative questions are beyond the limit of analysis. Moreover, one need not *do* analysis to be able to apply the results of some perceptive analysis. In the preceding example, we did not analyze disagreements as, for instance, we did work through the analysis of the subjective dimension of explanation. Rather, we merely took the fruits of Stevenson's analytic labors and applied them to a context relevant to education. The moral here is that the results of analysis are not limited to use by technical philosophers of education only, but may be used intelligently by any educator if such analyses can be seen to have relevance to his or her own sphere of educational interests and problems. In this way, this introduction to analysis offers more than an acquaintance with a special way of thinking about education; it invites educators to make practical use of the abundance of contemporary analytic writings in philosophy of education that are available on all sides.

It should be clear from this introduction to philosophical analysis that the distinctions developed and dealt with, the assumptions uncovered, and the use of concrete examples to force abstract ideas

---

8   For an extended analytic treatment of the mix of value and factual considerations that go into sound educational policymaking, see Donna H. Kerr, *Educational Policy: An Analysis, Structure, and Justification* (New York: McKay, 1976).

into meaningful contexts offer a very direct route for the application of analytic theorizing to educational practicing. Our concerns were not remote, but dealt directly with ideas that *are* used to guide practice. I firmly believe that one of the greatest advantages to the use of analysis in education is this proximity of the types of problems and ideas dealt with to the down-to-earth, everyday enterprise of educating. Moreover, the impatient attitude of the analytic philosopher toward fuzzy thinking and vague ideas, should it be caught by many practicing educators, could prove to be the single most important contribution of philosophy of education to educational practice today. To be told that students should learn by discovery or that one should teach the "structure" of the subject is not to get answers to the practical questions of how and what to teach. Rather, such directives provide a context for asking some important prior questions, questions that will give practical meaning to these ideas. Discovery of what? Anything? Everything? What is discovery and how does learning by discovery differ from other kinds of learning? What is the structure of a subject? What criteria must be met by an element of a subject for it to count as part of the structure of that subject?

To make the language of education work, we must be clear about its intent and meaning and not be swayed only by its imagery and poetry. The analytic temperament and techniques should prove very useful to all practicing educators in getting them to think through with care and precision just what it is they are buying from theorists, and, more importantly, just what it is they're after and how best that might be achieved. As I have pointed out elsewhere, much of what goes on in good teaching occurs in the mind of the teacher long before he or she enters the classroom. It is precisely in this "thinking through" process that the techniques and results of analysis have most to offer the practicing educator.

THE LANGUAGE OF EDUCATION[9]

These are but a few of the potential practical applications of philosophical analysis to the business of education. I hope this book has helped people to come to appreciate the special qualities inherent in language and, most especially, in the language of education. In this book we have dealt exclusively with the *ordinary* language of education, which carries with it complex and assumed meanings,

---

9   The description of the "language of education" in this section is drawn from my paper, "The Passion to Teach," *Theory into Practice* 12, no. 1 (1973): 5–12. Used with permission of the publisher.

logical relations, and the potential for generating conceptual confusions. But, in complex formal educational systems such as ours, special and technical languages and sets of concepts also are developed to describe the functions, operations, and goals of our system. In psychology and the social sciences, the technical language is descriptive of the learning process, human interaction, and human development. In curriculum and methods, the special languages and concepts are more often prescriptive, pointing to desirable ways to educate. And, in the subject-matter areas, there are specialized ways to describe and think about a unique set of phenomena.

Thus, the language of education becomes complex, technical, and specialized. In fact, an important part of the process of training educators is getting them to learn and fully understand this complex language and the ideas and relationships it contains. The language of education then becomes the basic instrument used by teachers, curriculum makers, administrators, and theorists to plan and carry out the educational enterprise. Similarly, school innovations, theories of learning, methods of teaching, curriculum changes, and restatements of educational aims all are formulated in the language of education. The transmission and dispersion of these ideas throughout the entire educational system is dependent on the clarity and precision of their statement as well as on the ability of the recipient to understand and translate them into effective educational practice. In these ways, the language of education becomes one of the most important tools of the professional educator.

But, like any tool, the language of education may be used efficiently or inefficiently. This depends on the skill of the person using the tool and also on the quality of the tool itself. A dull knife is of no use to the skilled woodcarver and a sharp knife in the hands of a child is a dangerous instrument. Good educational ideas in the heads of educational theorists are of no use to the practicing teacher unless these ideas can be understood and successfully applied to the difficult task of educating the young. On the other hand, weak and vague ideas can be used by incompetent educators to hide their ineffectiveness behind an impressive veneer of fancy but empty words. In the right hands and heads, the language of education can become a powerful instrument for planning and promoting effective learning. But in unskilled hands and cloudy heads, the language of education becomes a refuge for the incompetent, who sometimes so impress us with their vocabulary that we foolishly assume they really know what they're doing.

Words have power, but languages are more than words. They are systems for imposing order on the world and for organizing ideas and relationships in our minds. A language system carries with it many unstated assumptions and beliefs about the world and our actions in it. The language of education shares these features of language in general. Thus, we find that some educational words have power—the power to redirect the procedures and purposes of educators. In the American progressive-education movement a generation ago and in our current concern to repair faulty educational processes and institutions, such words as "open classroom," "child-centered education," "problem solving," "learning by doing," "inquiry education," "behavioral objectives," "alternative schooling," and many others provide the power to radically alter educational activities.

But words of the sort mentioned do not possess such power in themselves. To attain their power, the total framework of the ideas these words represent must be fully understood by those who use them. Without such an understanding, many educational words become empty slogans; or, even worse, they provide the license for doing anything under the protective blanket of their impressive names. In this way, educational abuses and failures can arise in what seems to be a reasonable and workable educational plan. But if the word is only as good as the idea behind it, we as educators should ask ourselves more frequently just what this or that educational term means. To what assumptions, values, theories, procedures, and strategies for teaching do these words commit us?

These are not questions only for philosophers; they are questions that must be constantly asked and answered by all educators, but most especially by teachers themselves. For, in the last analysis, an educational idea is powerful only if it is translated into practice in each and every classroom.

Theories, methods, directives, curricula, or suggestions issued by others can be of help to the teacher, but each teacher must make and understand and believe in his or her own plan for educating students; otherwise, any attempt at teaching will be mechanical and purposeless. With a functional grasp of the language of education, teachers can more fully understand the educational situation, more easily diagnose students' problems, more adequately plan effective teaching strategies, and more efficiently evaluate successes and failures.

To create this needed sensitivity to the language of education and to provide the opportunity for prospective teachers to construct their own conceptual maps, the approach to philosophy of education sketched in this book seems to be eminently suited. There are many limits to the approach called "philosophical analysis" and I have tried to point out some of them in this chapter, but there are also many uses for analysis in education of which no contemporary practicing educator ought to be ignorant. I invite my readers to continue this journey of the mind by searching out other relevant works of analytic philosophers and, more importantly, by examining their own ideas about education relentlessly until they truly make *good sense*.

Epilogue:
The pedagogy of
analytic-skills
development

7

The topics, techniques, and strategies dealt with in this introduction to the analysis of educational concepts have been culled from a wealth of contemporary analytic writings. Our treatment of them has been simplified in order to achieve the major purpose of this book: to acquaint the reader with analytic approaches to thinking about educational ideas. Ordinarily, it is a lot easier to acquaint people with a set of ideas then it is to get them to master new skills. Thus, I would assume that few would walk away from reading this book without having grasped the distinction between knowing *how* and knowing *that* or without a notion of a "vehicle" sense of subject matter or the "intentional-rational" sense of teaching. But it is possible that merely naming, describing, and illustrating various analytic techniques and strategies is not sufficient to ensure that readers will acquire even minimal competence in their use. To deal with this possibility, I have added this epilogue, in the belief that an introduction to analysis would be sorely deficient if it failed to provide a means to develop and practice the analytic skills substantively presented.

I have placed this pedagogy of analytic-skills development at the end of this volume for two reasons. First, it allows me to summarize the techniques and strategies dealt with in the book and, at the same time, provides a convenient source of information for people who wish to develop analytic skills on their own. I believe this is preferable to breaking up the text with extended summaries and exercises. Second, adding this epilogue enables me to draw attention to a major purpose of this book: to provide a vehicle for the teaching and learning of some skills in thinking. So often textbooks do not reflect their intended pedagogy when, by definition, that is their very purpose for being.

This has been a book with a dual focus, one on substance and one on methods. Thus, this epilogue can best be used to highlight and underscore the methodological dimension, now that the substantive discussions are finished. To this end, I have organized the epilogue in a way that should facilitate its use for analytic-skills development. This can be done either by using relevant parts of this epilogue as end-of-chapter activities or as end-of-book summary, review, and practice projects. In the sections that follow, the "Review" suggestions are designed to help people look for and recognize exemplars of the strategies or techniques identified in the main text; the "Exercises" are designed to provide opportunities for simplified directed practice; and the suggested "Practice" projects cap the pedagogical enterprise by challenging a would-be learner to apply the techniques or strategies creatively with a minimum of structured prompting. What follows, then, are a set of suggestions, activities to help one engage in *trying* to develop analytic skill. The particular suggestions have been tested and refined over the years with students and colleagues, but one should feel free to invent one's own vehicles for learning should these not work.

The assumption here is that to *learn how* to do something, one must first *try* to do it. As my young daughter once proudly said, "Practice makes good!" One should not expect perfection, mastery, or even competence from doing what is suggested here. But, with a bit of hard work and some good self, peer, and/or instructor critique, one should be able to acquire an appreciation of analysis as a skilled craft; a sensitive attitude toward ideas, concepts, and meanings; and a beginner's facility with the three strategies demonstrated in this book. For those willing to try, the sense of accomplishment will be its own reward.

LOCATING THE FIELD OF PLAY

Beginners not only have a hard time focusing on analytic techniques and strategies, they also have difficulty recognizing the boundaries of proper areas of application for philosophical analysis. We have already said that clarifying concepts is not the same as ascertaining facts or making value judgments.[1] To give you a better idea of just what this means, an extended analogy with games may be useful. Playing tennis (doing analysis) is not like playing football (doing science, or math, or history); they are not even played on the same sort of "field." In fact, football would hardly be the same game if played on a tennis court. The basic moves in football—pass, kick, run—are quite different from those in tennis, as are the rules, penalties, and the scoring schemes of the two games.

Getting a feel for what the analytic "game" is about requires that one be able to locate the field of play, see the object of the game, and recognize the basic moves. Just as a newcomer to the football stadium would not be able to make much sense of the activities observed, so one watching analysis being done would find the process difficult to understand. As in football, one must know where the game is being played, what its object is, and what the players are doing. This section of the epilogue is aimed at providing ways to get this general perspective on philosophical analysis as an activity.

There are a number of things one can do to help locate "the field of play." Imagine you have just arrived in a very strange land where all communication is carried on by means of written single statements or questions. Before any response can be given or another statement added to a message, the listener must put each prior communication into the correct one of three colored containers or else all communication stops. You watch the inhabitants talking and see the following sorts of messages going into the black container: "There are over five thousand courses at this college." "Is it raining still?" "The rug in my room is brown." Into the white container go these: "The sunset is beautiful." "Is the school system here good?" "Chemistry is more important than poetry." And into the gray container go these: "Rote memorization isn't learning." "Is teaching a profession?" "That's just lecturing, not teaching."

Into which containers would you expect these messages to go?

a) How many people live here?

b) Is the food good?

c) Are your citizens free?

d) It took two days to get here.

e) It's wrong to ask too many questions.

f) Communication is an art.

---

1   Except perhaps in a very strained sense of these terms.

Think about it and try to categorize the messages yourself before looking at the footnote below.[2] Now, if you have caught on to the language game of this strange land, you could go right on playing it yourself on an intuitive basis without ever trying to construct rules for playing it or giving names to the three containers. But the point of this little exercise is to get you to see that the grey container marks "the field of play" for analysis, so we will have to do some naming and sketching of rules to help you understand what this means.

Black-container messages we ordinarily call *factual* or *empirical*—they can be checked (5,000 or 5,001 courses) or answered (still raining?) by ascertaining states of affairs in the world. White-container messages are harder to ascertain because they deal with values and value judgments (a *good* school system; poetry is *better* than chemistry) and because value messages aren't read off directly from the way the world is, but are dependent on human valuings and value systems. Gray-container items may look like either black or white message units, but they are first and foremost dependent on the ascertaining of *meaning* before fact or value considerations are possible. Thus, it is hard to determine if someone is free unless you know what the questioner means by "free." Free from physical restraint? Free within the laws or without laws? Free to leave, free to follow one's conscience, etc.? The same holds true with the concepts of "learning," "profession," "teaching," and "art." Unless we know what *meaning* these terms carry, it is difficult to answer the questions or to agree or disagree with the statements made about them. In fact, analytically speaking, each requires that the prior conceptual question, "What is the meaning of x?" be asked and answered before one can go on to consider the substantive content of the message. And this is how the game of analysis gets to be played in the field of concepts and not on factual or evaluational terrain.

"What is the definition of education?" first requires clarification of what is *meant* by the question, just as does the question, "Must an educator have an aim?" or, "What is the most fruitful conception of subject matter?" Often doing this requires use of that handy analytic technique called making distinctions. If we recognize that a term may have more than one basic meaning, it behooves us to identify and compare those meanings and to say some such thing as, "If you

---

2   Black container, a and d; white container, b and e; gray container, c and f. The use of imagined or invented cases is another basic technique of analysis; see John Wilson's description of it in *Thinking with Concepts* (London: Cambridge University Press, 1963), pp 32–33. Also see his parallel discussion of the fact, value, concept distinction in his book's first chapter, "The Business of Analysis."

mean *aim* (short-range goal), then having an aim is conceptually necessary to the meaning of being an educator; but if you mean *Aim* (long-range goal), then having an Aim is not logically essential, though it may be inspirationally useful and socially wise. The making of distinctions helps to make meaning clear and is an important basic maneuver on the analytic field of conceptual play. And the "game" *is* a serious one. It isn't just play. How we and others conceive of things and which meanings we take to be ours subtly but surely directs the course of what we and others do in the world of fact and value.

For those who would like some additional practice at locating the analytical field of play and in making simple distinctions, the following activities are suggested:

REVIEW
1. Look back through the text and locate some factual, valuational, and conceptual statements or questions. Look also for prior questions.

2. Make a list of some of the basic distinctions made in the text which you find useful.

EXERCISE
3. Add some simple statements or questions to the "black," "white," and "gray" imaginary containers described above. Can you ask prior questions of all your additions to the gray container? Do they lead straight off to any obvious distinctions?

4. From your list of distinctions from number 2 above, provide your own fresh examples to illustrate some of the more useful or interesting distinctions.

PRACTICE
5. Identify some educational idea important to you and try to formulate a conceptual statement or question relating to it which isn't, at least on the face of it, simply a factual or valuational one. Ask an appropriate prior question and try to make a distinction useful to understanding what is at issue in the original statement or question.

But just finding the stadium and being able to tell who's on the playing field and who's off and what counts as the beginning of the game is not yet to be prepared to watch the plays develop as variations on the basic moves and strategies employed by the players. The subsequent sections in this epilogue are devoted to explicating some of the basic analytic moves and strategies. Before leaving this already somewhat strained game analogy, it may be useful to describe them briefly.

As we have already noted, the point of the game of analysis is to clarify conceptual issues in a search for a conceptual perspective that will be helpful in theorizing, practicing, or problem solving. Three basic strategies for doing that are outlined in this book. Each aims at reaching a certain kind of clarification by asking a certain kind of prior question. A generic-type analysis aims at finding the necessary conceptual features or properties of a thing and tries to answer the question, "What is an X?" or, "What features make something an X?" For instance, we might ask what conceptual features makes a statement factual or empirical in nature and start off by noting that the feature of being either true or false in terms of having some relationship to the world is taken to be part of what we mean by saying that a statement is empirical.

A differentiation-type analysis aims at identifying and separating basic senses or meanings of something and thereby illuminates more fully the topography of some conceptual domain. This is done by asking questions such as, "What are the different uses of the term X?" (Aim, long-range; aim, short-range) or, "What are the various types of X?" (for example, identifying types of messages as factual, valuational, and conceptual) and then seeking the distinguishing marks that separate these ideas.[3]

Finally, conditions-type analyses result from asking prior questions like, "What are the contextual conditions governing the proper use of the term X?" or, "What are the contextual conditions under which it would be correct to say that someone is X-ing?" For instance, the proper use of the term "seeing" in its literal sense requires the presence of a physical object, sufficient light, eyes opened, etc. If any of these conditions were missing from a context in which it was claimed that seeing really occurred, we wouldn't know how such a claim could possibly be made by a person who speaks the language correctly.

These three strategies of analysis have been sketched and exemplified in earlier chapters. The sections that follow provide summaries of their forms, further illumination of their structures by means of simple examples, and practice suggestions for those who would try to gain some skill in using them.

---

3   Making distinctions is what this strategy is about, but it is more than merely making a simple distinction, as will be shown in the fuller subsequent discussion of this strategy in this epilogue.

GENERIC-TYPE ANALYSIS

In the spirit of analysis, let's take a simple concrete example to illustrate the strategy of a generic-type analysis. Imagine that the concept in need of clarification is the geometric term "square." Our generic-type prior question is then, "What features must a two-dimensional figure have to be called a square?" The first step in the strategy is to draw from your general knowledge of standard cases of squares some potentially necessary features, such as: (1) Must have four sides. Now there are two ways to test this (and the other) feature(s). First, for *necessity:* Can you draw a square that doesn't have four sides? If not, then having four sides seems to be a *necessary* characteristic of squares. Can you draw a square without using ink? If yes, then having "inked lines" doesn't seem to be a necessary feature of all squares. Second, we can test for *sufficiency:* Can you draw a four-sided figure that isn't a square? Yes: ⬭ . Such a counterexample figure may suggest the need for some additional necessary feature, like: (2) Opposite sides must be parallel. Can you remove this feature from a square and still have a square? If not, then it is *necessary.* Are these two necessary characteristics *sufficient?* Not if you can draw a figure that has four sides and also has opposite sides parallel which isn't a square. Can you? Yes: ☐ . Therefore, we need to add: (3) All sides must be equal. Test for necessity: Can you remove this feature and still have a square? No? Then, test for sufficiency: Can you find a counterexample, a figure that has all three necessary characteristics, but still isn't a square? Yes: ▱. Therefore, we also need: (4) Internal angles must be right angles. It would seem that no figure with these four characteristics is possible without being a square. They are *sufficient.*[4] Nor could any figure count as a square if it failed to have any one of these *necessary* features.

Unfortunately, not all generic-type analyses are as simple and as straightforward as is this one, even though the moves and guiding purpose are essentially the same—for example, the concepts of baldness and middle-age are considerably less precise than is the concept of a square! But, in general, this form of analytic strategy loosely follows a set of rules which includes: the drawing of features from standard models of X (squares); the testing of the features (equal sides, parallel sides, right angles) for necessity by trying to remove each one of them from a standard case to see if each is absolutely essential; testing for sufficiency by searching for a counterexample that contains all the features identified to that point, but which

4   Of course, the good Euclidean would say that four equal sides and one right angle are sufficient to guarantee that the figure must be a square.

clearly is not an instance of X (rectangles, parallelograms); and revising the features requirement or adding to the list of features to block the force of the counterexample.[5]

This was the type of strategy used in examining the concept of a discipline in Chapter 2. It is important to see that, even though a particular mode of analysis may not be entirely successful, as in the case of attempting to clarify the concept of a discipline, the general aim of analysis may still be achieved. Clarification of the meaning of the term by pointing to its inherent vagueness should inform any discussion in which the concept plays an essential role. For those who would seek to gain a better grasp of this strategy of generic-type analysis and would like to practice using it, the following activities are suggested.

REVIEW   1. Reread the simplified "square" analysis above until you feel that you can clearly see the moves being made in terms of the strategy outlined.

2. Review the analysis of the concept of a discipline in Chapter 2 and try to sketch in short form the generic-type moves made there.

EXERCISE   3. Try a simple generic-type analysis of the concept of "science" along these lines.[6] Use as your standard cases the scientific activities of biology, chemistry, or physics, and take as your clear contrary case the typical activities of a door-to-door vacuum salesman. Test these features:

   a) Provides causal explanations.

   b) Claims supported by empirical evidence.

   c) Results are useful in the practical world.

   d) (Add one or two additional features of your own.)

PRACTICE   4. Consider the question, "Is teaching a profession?" and ask the prior question, "What characteristics logically make any recognized profession a profession?" Do a generic-type analysis on the concept of a "profession" and then try to shed some light on

---

5   These "moves," as well as those of the other strategies of analysis, are depicted graphically in Fig. 7.1, pp. 108–109.

6   At least initially and for purposes of practice, don't get too seriously caught up in the substantive issues; just try to understand and imitate the moves.

the original question. For the purposes of this exercise, assume you have no problems with the meaning of teaching as an occupation.

5. In the chapter in which we demonstrated a generic-type analysis by examining the concept of a discipline, we also provided a *relational schema*, a *formula*, for displaying the "vehicle" sense of subject matter as the outcome of a differentiation-type analysis. Hoping not to confuse the reader here, I would like to suggest that one way to look at the formula "S teaches P x so that y" is as a generic-type sketch of the features essential to the conception of an "educational situation." In effect, it claims that proper application of the term "educational situation" requires these elements:

S, a teacher;

P, a pupil;

x, something to be learned; and

y, the educational point of the enterprise.

There are three things you might try to do with this way of looking at the formula:

a) Test its adequacy by noting the number of logical possibilities it provides for fitting all types of educational situations. Substitute a number of concrete examples or counterexamples into the formula.

b) Critique the formula and show its inadequacy as a generic analysis of the concept of "an educational situation."

c) Develop your own relational schema which illuminates the conceptual dimension of anything we would ordinarily call "an educational situation" and which focuses attention on a conceptual point you wish to make.[7] I used the formula to display a concept of subject matter. There are other descriptions of the basic meaning of the concept "an educational situa-

7   It is important to recognize that ordinarily analyses are done to serve some end or purpose beyond the obvious one of clarifying a concept—for example, to solve a problem, to more fully understand an issue, to display a set of logically possible options, etc.

tion" useful for other purposes; for example, "S interacts with P via x with the result that P learns x," or, "Environment E produces the learning of x by P," etc.

DIFFERENTIATION-TYPE ANALYSIS

Once again, we will begin with an intentionally simple example to display the moves in the strategy of a differentiation-type analysis. Let us begin with the undifferentiated general concept of "material object." Now, obviously, that term can refer to anything and everything and were we to do a generic-type analysis on it, we might list features like having visible form, having mass, being perceivable by means of the senses, etc. But let us suppose that our conceptual puzzle is not simply to determine what the concept refers to. Rather, we sense the need to try to find some way to discriminate among the various types of items it refers to so that we won't be dealing with toads, tomatoes, and totem poles as if they were similar sorts of things. People are material objects in one sense, of course, but surely they are different from dandelions or doorknobs. Intuitively we sense these differences and, even with these few examples, we may be able to group them in some useful pattern. Doorknobs are much more like totem poles than like people, toads, or dandelions, in that the latter three all share the properties of being living things whereas doorknobs and totem poles do not. But toads and people are more alike than are toads and dandelions or people and dandelions, because dandelions are vegetable matter and toads and people are not. In short, then, it would seem that we have arrived at the simple, party-game category system of *animal, vegetable,* or *mineral* as a way to differentiate between all manner of material objects. We could test these categories, of course, by various examples to see if they do have the range that we claim for them—that with this typology we can classify each and every thing we call a material object; and also to see if they are mutually exclusive—nothing that is a material object can be more than one type of thing at a time.

While we seem to be able to put things easily into one or the other of these categories, however, we have said nothing of *why* they go into one or the other, and so have not made clear the *grounds* for our classification. Surely we are paying attention to the *distinguishing marks* possessed by each of so many material objects, marks that allow us to easily catagorize them in these ways.

What might these telltale "markers" be? Rocks and doorknobs neither feed nor reproduce themselves, but, obviously, people, toads, and dandelions do. These two marks, nutritive and reproductive

capacities,[8] mark the border between animate and inanimate substance, but they don't separate animal from vegetable. Aristotle
comes to the rescue with the distinguishing marks of "locomotion,"
"sensation," and "thought" for animals and he reserves the final distinguishing mark of "reason" for humans. Thus, we can see the
makings of a hierarchy here which could cap off this differentiation-
type analysis of the concept of a "material object" by sketching a *relational map* of these classes, were we to fully flesh it out and accept
Aristotle's distinguishing marks.

Let's now stand back and see what was done in the above analysis. Even though the doing of a differentiation-type analysis is seldom so easy an undertaking, this simple case will help us better see
what this type of analysis is about. We began with a question quite
different from the sort that guides a generic-type analysis. We did
not ask, "What are the concept's generic features?" Instead, within
some general class of things called "material objects," we sought a
conceptual means for differentiating between the use of the same
term to refer to different sorts of things. After coming up with some
intuitively different examples (toads, totem poles, dandelions, and
people), we compared and contrasted them in an attempt to get a preliminary grouping or category system for them (animal, vegetable,
mineral). Then we tested the range and adequacy of that system (no
material objects not able to be classified by it) and, finally, we sought
the key marks or characteristics by which each category in the
system was distinguished from any other (nutritive, reproductive,
sensation, thought, reason). We even noted that the system could be
seen to take a relational form (hierarchy) and not just be perceived as
an unordered aggregate.

We can see now that making simple distinctions is one thing, and
that doing a differentiation-type analysis is a much more complex
and ambitious undertaking. Henderson not only tried to make clear
distinctions between uses of the term "subject matter," but also
sought to refine more fully our concept of subject matter as knowledge. I continued that project in the same way with the addition of a
"vechicle" sense of subject matter. There is much more to mapping
the logical terrain of a general concept than making a few simple distinctions.[9] For those who would like to work up to trying a dif-

---

8   Thanks to Aristotle!

9   Thomas F. Green's "A Topology of the Teaching Concept," is an excellent example of a sophisticated application of a differentiation-type
analysis. It goes far beyond making simple distinctions and provides a
good relational mapping of the family of concepts attached to the idea of
getting someone to learn something.

ferentiation-type analysis, the following suggestions and activities may be of some use:

REVIEW 1. Review the simplified "material object" differentiation-type analysis in this section until you feel that you understand the flow and basic moves of the strategy.

2. Review either or both the subject matter and types of knowing discussions in Chapters 2 and 3, looking for and noting two "moves":

a) types and categories identified;

b) distinguishing marks identified.

EXERCISE 3. Using the review in number 2 above, do the following:

a) Try to test via example and counterexample the range and adequacy of the types of knowing analyses.

b) Try to find missing distingushing marks or additional legitimate categories.

4. Using the black, white, and gray container discussion in the epilogue section, "Locating the Field of Play," try to find distinguishing marks for the fact, value, and concept category system.

PRACTICE 5. Do a differentiation-type analysis on the concept of "learning" either as a parallel to the knowing *how* and knowing *that* formulation (noting where knowing and learning differ) or on some other dimension of the concept of learning—e. g., product-process, intentional activity-passive result, etc. It might be helpful to begin with the question, "Is there more than one type or meaning of learning?"

CONDITIONS-TYPE ANALYSIS

Sometimes the concept we are puzzling over is bothersome to us not because it has multiple senses—we may have already located a special sense to analyze—but because a generic-type strategy doesn't seem useful or even possible. Model or standard cases from which to draw potential generic features don't seem to be readily available to us. Unlike the situation in which we knew straight off that math and science count as "disciplines" and law and medicine as "professions," we might not be so sure about what would count as a model case of "teaching," "explaining," or "understanding." In fact, our very problem often is to find conditions that would have to be met by *any* case to count as a standard case and thus warrant a proper use of the concept in the context defined by the conditions identified. The point of departure for a conditions-type analysis, therefore, is to puzzle over the *context* appropriate for the use of the concept and not so much over its more acontextual generic meaning or its different senses.[10]

To illustrate the moves of this strategy, let's take the simple literal sense of the term "seeing"[11] and ask the conceptual question, "What are the logical conditions for properly using the term "seeing"? Obviously, one must have eyes to see with. Moreover, one's eyes need to be in working order and need to be open, and there needs to be light. Let us call all of this "eyes condition" to make the conceptual point that seeing logically requires functioning eyes as a necessary condition. But we also know that one cannot now claim to see Uncle Ben who is 500 miles away in Boston or to see love or leprechauns or the other side of the door if it is closed. To make a proper claim to see something, we need to be assured that it is spatially present, in our field of vision, and that it must be something in the "material object" sense of things. We will call this the "material-object-in-view condition." Now, whenever these two contextual conditions are met, it would seem that we could say with surity that someone has seen something. Even if we are wrong about *what* is seen—for example, mistaking a wire for a snake in the grass—it still would seem to be the literal seeing of *something*, and hence a case of seeing in the literal sense.

But are these two conditions sufficient for the proper use of the term "seeing"? Imagine being a hunter, eyes open, plenty of light, etc. and you are looking for a deer. Your trusted guide points in a direction and you train your eyes on the spot. Indeed, neatly camouflaged against the forest background, a deer stands transfixed, staring right back at you—but you say you cannot see it. But we say that the "eye" and "material object" conditions have been met and so logically you *must* see it, at which point you become certain that

---

10   Though having some sense of both of these latter can usefully inform a conditions-type analysis.

11   The analysis in this section is drawn from my book: J. F. Soltis, *Seeing, Knowing, and Believing: A Study of the Language of Visual Perception* (London: George Allen and Unwin, 1966).

analytic philosophers will never make good hunters. What is clearly missing here is a lack of what we shall call the "discrimination" condition. If you cannot or did not pick something out of your field of vision, even though it is there to be seen, it makes little sense to say that you saw it. It is a bit like looking into an open jewelry box and saying, "I don't see my cufflinks" (which are right there in view), to which someone responds, "But you must because they are there." Logically, a discrimination condition is required for the proper use of the term "seeing," just as visual discrimination is empirically essential if you want to get about in the visual world effectively.

Thus ends our truncated analysis of "seeing." Once again, we should point to the moves made in this oversimplified version of the conditions-type analysis strategy. To start the analysis, we began with an obviously necessary condition fairly fully formulated. (If we had left out "eyes open" in our first formulation of the "eyes" condition, a closed-eyes example would have forced a revision of the condition and not a consideration of an additional and different condition.) Next, we sought an example in which the necessary condition holds, but the context is such that the phenomena (seeing of x) does not occur (love, leprechauns, and Uncle Ben), to test for sufficiency. Consideration of the impeding context variables (nonmaterial things, material object not in view) led to the formulation of an additional necessary condition ("material object"). These conditions were then tested in combination for sufficiency and, when found lacking, forced the need for the "discrimination" condition. Other examples were imagined until no conceivable change in context seemed possible to call into question the necessity or sufficiency of the conditions identified.

I know it is easier said than done, but for those who would like to give the conditions-type analysis strategy a try, the following activities may prove helpful:

REVIEW   1. Review the simplified "seeing" analysis in this section until you have a feel for the moves of the strategy of a conditions-type analysis.

2. Reread the section in Chapter 4, "Conditions for a Satisfying Explanation," and do a strategy sketch of the analysis there by listing in order each condition and the example(s) used to test the condition and force revision or consideration of another condition as the analysis develops.

EXERCISE   3. Start a conditions-type analysis of the concept "having an opportunity" by taking as the first condition that "a state of affairs exists which makes x possible for S to do." Try to think of a contextual example which will force the consideration of a second condition that "S must 'see' that x is possible for S to do." Are other conditions needed to complete the analysis?

PRACTICE   4. Try your hand at a conditions-type analysis by answering one or more of the following questions: What must be true or what conditions must hold to say that

a) P has given the right answer?

b) P is studying?

c) P is obeying the rule x?

d) P is practicing?

CONCLUSION

For those who have made it this far, may I suggest going back to the beginning of the text and rereading it. So many things can be missed on the first reading simply because you don't yet know what you are reading for. Especially when emphasis is on technique, skill, and strategy, one can easily miss seeing what one has not yet learned to see, just as a child might walk through a gallery of skillful still-life paintings and see only flowers and bowls of fruit, completely missing the artistry represented.

In any case, whether you go back or not, there is no returning to a more naive stance toward the world of language once you have gotten a feeling for the important role concepts play in our everyday dealings with each other and once you have acquired some tools with which to probe the conceptual dimension and do your own thinking. For those who might like to go on, I hope that Fig. 7.1, a schematic sketch of the three strategies described in the epilogue, will serve as a useful map. Figure 7.1 appears on pages 108–109. In addition, a somewhat simplified version of the figure appears on the front endpaper of the book. While no simple recipe is possible for directing different modes of analytic thinking, these descriptors may serve as useful guides until you can do analysis flexibly and intelligently on your own. Good luck!

Fig. 7.1 THREE ANALYTIC STRATEGIES

GENERIC TYPE

NATURE OF THE ANALYTIC SITUATION	Undisputed model case(s) of the concept X are readily available, but generic features shared by model species are not clearly spelled out.
FORM OF PRIOR QUESTION	What features must x have to be an X?

MOVES

I.	1. Select standard or model cases and clear contrary cases of X.
II.	2. Draw potentially necessary features from clear standard cases.
III.	3. Test: Use examples and counterexamples (contrary cases) to test for necessity and sufficiency.
IV.	4. Keep, modify, or reject the feature(s) on the basis of the test(s).

INTENDED RESULT	A clearer idea of what is essential to being an X.

DIFFERENTIATION TYPE	CONDITIONS TYPE
The concept X seems to have more than one standard meaning and their identities and the basis for differentiating between them aren't clear.	Undisputed model cases don't seem to be readily available and standard instances of the concept X can easily be made noninstances by changing a context condition.
What are the basic (different) meanings of X?	Under what context conditions would it be true to say that X is present or that C is Xing?
1. Search for dominant standard uses of the concept by means of examples.	1. Identify a good candidate for being a necessary condition of X happening or X being present in a situation.
2. Intuitively classify or categorize the uses into types. Any missing types?	2. By altering the context, try to find an example where the condition holds, but X or Xing is not present.
3. Search for distinguishing marks of each type which can be used to clearly separate types.	3. Revise or modify the condition to meet the context problem or tease out from the altered context another condition and test it (as in no. 2).
4. Test the typology developed by means of examples and counterexamples; schematize relations if possible.	4. Test the necessity and sufficiency of the conditions arrived at.
A clearer idea of the logical terrain covered by different meanings of a concept.	A clearer idea of the contextual dimension of a concept's meaning.

Bibliography

The topics dealt with in *An Introduction to the Analysis of Educational Concepts* have been selected from a wealth of contemporary analytic writings. The treatment of them has been simplified in order to achieve the major purposes of this book—to acquaint the reader with the analytic approach to thinking about educational ideas in both its substantive and its methodological dimensions. In this bibliography, I have selected some more advanced analytic writings to add to the books and articles already dealt with in the text, so that the initiate may gain a broader sense of the literature now available in this field and, moveover, so that he or she may see that what was said about the topics dealt with in these pages is hardly the last word. I must emphasize that this is a *selected* bibliography, and that my selections were guided mainly by the purposes to which this book has been directed. No attempt has been made to be exhaustive; some very good analytic selections may have been omitted. My primary intention was to provide a handy list of sources which might be used for such activities as class discussions, term-paper topics, or other forms of practice, review, research, and involvement in philosophical analysis beyond what was dealt with in this book.

INTRODUCTORY WORKS

Arnstine, Donald. *Philosophy of Education; Learning and Schooling.* New York: Harper & Row, 1967.

Beck, Clive. *Educational Philosophy and Theory: An Introduction.* Boston: Little, Brown, 1974.

Brown, L. M. *General Philosophy in Education.* New York: McGraw-Hill, 1966.

Ennis, Robert H. *Logic in Teaching.* Englewood Cliffs, N.J.: Prentice-Hall, 1969.

Green, Thomas F. *The Activities of Teaching.* New York: McGraw-Hill, 1971.

Gribble, James. *Introduction to Philosophy of Education.* Boston: Allyn and Bacon, 1969.

Hirst, Paul H., and Richard S. Peters. *The Logic of Education.* New York: Humanities Press, 1971.

McClellan, James E. *Philosophy of Education.* Englewood Cliffs, N.J.: Prentice-Hall, 1976.

O'Connor, D. J. *An Introduction to the Philosophy of Education.* London: Routledge and Kegan Paul, 1957.

Peters, R. S. *Ethics and Education.* London: Allen & Unwin, 1966. (American abridged edition: Glenview, Ill.: Scott, Foresman, 1967.)

Scheffler, Israel. *The Language of Education.* Springfield, Illinois: Charles C. Thomas, 1960.

Wilson, John. *Thinking with Concepts.* London: Cambridge University Press, 1963.

ANTHOLOGIES AND COLLECTIONS*

Archambault, Reginald D., ed. *Philosophical Analysis and Education.* New York: Humanities Press, 1965.

Bandman, Bertram, and Robert S. Guttchen, eds. *Philosophical Essays on Teaching.* New York: Lippincott, 1969.

Chazan, Barry I., and J. F. Soltis. *Moral Education.* New York: Teachers College Press, 1974.

---

* Perhaps the two best continuing vehicles for underwriting collections which include good analytic papers are the independently published proceedings of the philosophy of education societies of both North America and of Great Britain.

Dearden, R. F., P. H. Hirst, and R. S. Peters. *Education and the Development of Reason.* London: Routledge and Kegan Paul, 1972.

Hirst, Paul H. *Knowledge and the Curriculum.* Boston: Routledge and Kegan Paul, 1974.

Komisar, B. Paul, and J. Macmillan, eds. *Psychological Concepts in Education.* Chicago: Rand McNally, 1968.

Langford, Glenn, and D. J. O'Connor, eds. *New Essays in the Philosophy of Education.* Boston: Routledge and Kegan Paul, 1973.

Macmillan, Charles James Barr, and Thomas W. Nelson, eds. *Concepts of Teaching; Philosophical Essays.* Chicago: Rand McNally, 1968.

Martin, Jane R., ed. *Readings in the Philosophy of Education: A Study of Curriculum.* Rockleigh, N.J.: Allyn and Bacon, 1970.

Peters, Richard S. *Authority, Responsibility, and Education.* London: George Allen and Unwin, 1959.

————, ed. *The Concept of Education.* London: Routledge and Kegan Paul, 1967.

————, ed. *The Philosophy of Education.* London: Oxford University Press, 1973.

Scheffler, Israel, ed. *Philosophy and Education: Modern Readings.* 2d ed. Boston: Allyn and Bacon, 1966.

————. *Reason and Teaching.* Indianapolis: Bobbs-Merrill, 1973.

Smith, B. Othanel, and R. H. Ennis, eds. *Language and Concepts in Education.* Chicago: Rand McNally, 1961.

Smith, Ralph A., ed. *Aesthetic Concepts and Education.* Urbana: University of Illinois Press, 1970.

Snook, Ivan, ed. *Concepts of Indoctrination: Philosophical Essays.* London: Routledge and Kegan Paul, 1972.

Walton, J., and J. Kuethe, eds. *The Discipline of Education.* Madison, Wisconsin: University of Wisconsin Press, 1963.

GENERAL WORKS AND MONOGRAPHS

Ayer, A. J. *The Problem of Knowledge.* Harmondsworth, England: Penguin Books, Ltd., 1956.

Dray, William. *Laws and Explanations in History.* London: Oxford University Press, 1957.

Hardie, C. D. *Truth and Fallacy in Educational Theory.* New York: TC Press, 1962.

Kazepides, A. C. *The Autonomy of Education*. Athens, Greece: National Centre of Social Research, 1973.

Kerr, Donna H. *Educational Policy: Analysis, Structure, and Justification*. New York: McKay, 1976.

Martin, Jane R. *Explaining, Understanding and Teaching*. New York: McGraw-Hill, 1970.

Peters, Richard S. *Education as Initiation*. London: Evans Bros., Ltd., 1964.

_____. *Ethics and Education*. London: Allen and Unwin, Ltd., 1966.

Pratte, Richard. *The Public School Movement*. New York: McKay, 1973.

Ryle, Gilbert. *The Concept of Mind*. London: Hutchinson's University Library, 1949.

Scheffler, Israel. *The Conditions of Knowledge*. Glenview, Illinois: Scott, Foresman, 1965.

Soltis, Jonas F. *Seeing, Knowing, and Believing*. London: Allen and Unwin, Ltd., 1966.

Steinberg, Ira S. *Educational Myths and Realities*. Reading, Mass.: Addison-Wesley, 1968.

White, J. P. *Towards a Compulsory Curriculum*. London: Routledge and Kegan Paul, 1973.

Williamson, William B. *Language and Concepts in Christian Education*. Philadelphia: Westminster Press, 1970.

Wilson, John. *The Assessment of Morality*. Windsor, Berks, England: NFER Publishing Co., 1973.

_____. *Education in Religion and the Emotions*. London: Heinemann Educational Group, 1972.

_____. *Language and the Pursuit of Truth*. Cambridge: Cambridge University Press, 1969.

_____. *Philosophy and Educational Research*. Berks, England: National Foundation for Educational Research in England and Wales, 1972.

_____. *Practical Methods of Moral Education*. London: Heinemann. New York: Crane, Russak & Co., 1972.

ARTICLES AND PAPERS

Andris, James F. " 'Person X Is Teaching.' " *The Proceedings of the Philosophy of Education Society*, 1971.

Archambault, Reginald D. "Criteria for Success in Moral Instruction." *Harvard Educational Review* 33 (Fall 1963).

_____. "Manner in Education." *The Proceedings of the Philosophy of Education Society*, 1968.

_____. "The Concept of Need and Its Relation to Certain Aspects of Educational Theory." *Harvard Educational Review* 27 (Winter 1957).

_____. "Three Observations about Language." *Educational Theory* 13 (April 1963).

Atherton, Margaret. "Discovery as a Method of Teaching." *The Proceedings of the Philosophy of Education Society*, 1974.

Beck, Clive. "Knowing That, Knowing How to, Knowing to, and Knowing How." *The Proceedings of the Philosophy of Education Society*, 1968.

_____. "The Discipline of Education." *The Proceedings of the Philosophy of Education Society*, 1970.

Benedict-Gill, Diane. "A Subject Matter Description of Moral Education." *Educational Theory* 25 (Spring 1975).

Benson, Thomas L. "On Making Offers that Can't Be Refused." *Educational Theory* 24 (Summer 1974).

Berger, M. I. "Doing Things with the Concept of Teaching." *The Proceedings of the Philosophy of Education Society*, 1968.

_____. "Philosophic Method and Educational Concepts." *The Proceedings of the Philosophy of Education Society*, 1972.

_____. "Philosophizing about Teaching: Some Reconsiderations on Teaching as Act and Enterprise." *Studies in Philosophy and Education* 6 (1968).

Berson, Robert. "The Educational Situation and the Realm of Values." *Educational Theory* 25 (Spring 1975).

Brauner, Charles J. "Dearden Against Play." *The Proceedings of the Philosophy of Education Society*, 1976.

Broudy, Harry S. "Mastery." In *Language and Concepts in Education*, ed. by B. O. Smith and R. H. Ennis. Chicago: Rand McNally, 1961.

_____. "On Knowing With." *The Proceedings of the Philosophy of Education Society*, 1970.

_____. "The Role of Analysis in Educational Philosophy." *Educational Theory* 14 (October 1964).

Brown, Marcus. "Knowing and Learning." *Harvard Educational Review* 31 (Winter 1961).

Cambell, Colin. "A Comment on Whether Teaching Implies Learning." *Harvard Educational Review* 35 (Winter 1965).

Castell, A. "Two Senses of 'Learn.' " *University of Oregon School of Education Curriculum Bulletin* 20 (1964).

Chazan, Barry. "The Limits of 'Philosophy and Education.' " *Educational Philosophy and Theory,* April 1971.

Cheng-Whatt Koh, Jolly. "Jones Is Teaching." *The Proceedings of the Philosophy of Education Society,* 1976.

_____. "Paula Has Learned." *The Proceedings of the Philosophy of Education Society,* 1975.

Cochrane, Don. "Teaching and Creativity: A Philosophical Analysis." *Educational Theory* 25 (Winter 1975).

Cooper, B. A. "Peters' Concept of Education." *Educational Philosophy and Theory,* October 1973.

Cooper, David E. "Intentions and Indoctrination." *Educational Philosophy and Theory,* March 1973.

Crittenden, Brian. "Aims, Intentions and Purposes in Teaching and Educating." *Educational Theory* 24 (1974).

_____. "Teaching, Educating, and Indoctrinating." *Educational Theory* 28 (1968).

Daniels, Le Roi, and Shirley Parkinson. "Role X'ing and Moral Education—Some Conceptual Speculations." *Educational Theory* 26 (Fall 1976).

Dearden, R. F. "Competition in Education." *Proceedings of the Philosophy of Education Society of Great Britain* 6 (January 1972): 119–133.

_____. "Education and the Ethics of Belief." *British Journal of Educational Studies* 22 (1974): 5–17.

Dietl, Paul. "Teaching, Learning, and Knowing." *Educational Philosophy and Theory* 5 (October 1973).

_____. "The Irrelevance of Philosophy to Moral Education." *The Proceedings of the Philosophy of Education Society,* 1971.

Diller, Ann. " 'Teaching Moral Rules': A Preliminary Analysis." *The Proceedings of the Philosophy of Education Society,* 1975.

Edel, Abraham. "Analytic Philosophy of Education at the Cross-Roads." *Educational Theory* 22 (1972).

Elliott, R. K. "Versions of Creativity." *Proceedings of the Philosophy of Education Society of Great Britain* 5 (July 1971): 139–152.

Ennis, Robert H. "A Concept of Critical Thinking." *Harvard Educational Review* 32 (Winter 1962).

_____. "Equality of Educational Opportunity." *Educational Theory* 26 (Winter 1976).

_____. "Learning One's Responses and Only One's Responses." *Studies in Philosophy and Education.* 1, nos. 4 and 5 (November 1961).

Fen, Sing-Nan. " 'Knowing That' Rediscovered and Its Place in Pedagogy Reassigned." *Educational Theory* 16 (April 1966).

Fenstermacher, Gary D. "When Does Classroom Teaching Occur?" *The Proceedings of the Philosophy of Education Society,* 1974.

Flew, Antony. "Teaching and Testing." *The Proceedings of the Philosophy of Education Society,* 1973.

_____. "What Is Indoctrination?" *Studies in Philosophy and Education* 4, no. 2 (Spring 1966).

Fox, June T. "Epistemology, Psychology, and Their Relevance for Education in Bruner and Dewey." *Educational Theory* 19 (1969).

Freeman, Helen. "The Concept of Teaching." *Proceedings of the Philosophy of Education Society of Great Britain* 7 (January 1973): 7–25.

Gayer, Nancy, and M. F. Burnyeat. "Play and Pleasure." *Proceedings of the Philosophy of Education Society of Great Britain* 5 (January 1971): 29–36.

Goldstone, Peter J. "Philosophical Analysis and the Revolution." *The Proceedings of the Philosophy of Education Society,* 1970.

Green, K. "Intrinsic Motivation." *Proceedings of the Philosophy of Education Society of Great Britain* 6 (January 1972): 73–96.

Green, Thomas F. "A Topology of the Teaching Concept." *Studies in Philosophy and Education* 3, no. 4 (Winter 1964–65).

_____. "Teaching, Acting, and Behaving." *Harvard Educational Review* 34 (Fall 1964).

Gregory, I. M. M., and R. G. Woods. "Indoctrination." *Proceedings of the Philosophy of Education Society of Great Britain* 4 (January 1970): 77–105.

Guttchen, Robert S. "On Ethical Judgment and Education." *Educational Theory* 16 (April 1962).

_____. "The Logic of Practice." *Studies in Philosophy and Education* 7 (1969).

_____. "The Quest for Necessity." *Educational Theory* 16 (April 1966).

Halstead, Robert E. "Teaching for Understanding." *The Proceedings of the Philosophy of Education Society,* 1975.

Hamlyn, D. W. "The Concept of Development." *Proceedings of the Philosophy of Education Society of Great Britain* 9 (July 1975): 26–39.

Hamm, C. "The Role of Habit in Moral Education." *Educational Theory* 25 (Fall 1975).

Hardie, C. D. "Inductive Learning." *Educational Theory* 25 (Winter 1975).

_____. "Some Concepts in Education in the Light of Recent Philosophy." *Studies in Philosophy and Education* 2, no. 3 (Summer 1962).

_____. "The Philosophy of Education in a New Key." *Educational Theory* 10 (October 1960).

Hare, William F. "Appreciation as a Goal of Aesthetic Education." *Journal of Aesthetic Education* (April 1974).

_____. "Openness in Education." *The Proceedings of the Philosophy of Education Society,* 1974.

_____. "Responsibility and Rights in Contemporary Educational Theory." *Educational Theory* 22 (1972).

_____. "Teaching, Intention and Care." *Focus on Learning* 1 (1971).

_____. "The Teaching of Judgment." *British Journal of Educational Studies* 19.

_____. "Trying." *Kinesis* 3 (Fall 1970): 43–58.

Harrison, John L. "Modes of Knowing and Significant Meanings: Another Look at the Concept of Education." *The Proceedings of the Philosophy of Education Society,* 1974.

Hartland-Swann, John. "The Logical Status of 'Knowing That.' " *Analysis* 16 (April 1956).

Hay, William H., "On Green's Analysis of Teaching." *Studies in Philosophy and Education* 4, no. 2 (Fall 1965).

Haynes, Felicity. "Metaphor as Interactive." *Educational Theory* 25 (Summer 1975).

Henderson, Kenneth B. "Uses of 'Subject Matter.' " In *Language and Concepts in Education,* ed. by B. O. Smith and R. H. Ennis. Chicago: Rand McNally, 1961.

Heslep, Robert D. "Behavioral and Educational Thought." *Educational Philosophy and Theory*, March 1973.

_____. "Behavioral Definitions of Educational Terms." *The Proceedings of the Philosophy of Education Society*, 1973.

_____. "Mental States." *The Proceedings of the Philosophy of Education Society*, 1972.

_____. "Non-Physical Mental Acts as Educational Goals." *Educational Theory* 22 (1972).

_____. "Performed Actions and Acts as Logically Possible Teaching Objectives." *Studies in Philosophy and Education* 8 (1973).

_____. "Preferential Treatment and Compensatory Education." *Educational Theory* 26 (Spring 1976).

Hirst, Paul H. "Philosophy and Educational Theory." *British Journal of Educational Studies* 12 (November 1963).

Kapunan, Salvador C. "Teaching Implies Learning." *Educational Theory* 25 (Fall 1975).

Katz, M. S. "Two Views of 'Teaching People to Think.' " *Educational Theory* 26 (Spring 1976).

Kaufman, Abraham. "Teaching as an Intentional Serial Performance." *Studies in Philosophy and Education* 4, no. 4 (Summer 1966).

Kazepides, Anastasios C. "On the Nature of Philosophical Questions and the Function of Philosophy in Education." *The Proceedings of the Philosophy of Education Society*, 1970.

_____. "The Concept of Habit." *Educational Theory* 20 (1970).

_____. "The Grammar of 'Indoctrination.' " *The Proceedings of the Philosophy of Education Society*, 1973.

_____. "What is the Paradox of Moral Education?" *The Proceedings of the Philosophy of Education Society*, 1969.

Kennedy, Dale, "R. S. Peters' Concept of Character and the Criterion of Consistency for Action." *Educational Theory* 25 (Winter 1975).

Kerr, Donna H. "Analyses of 'Teaching.' " *Educational Philosophy and Theory* 6 (March 1974).

_____. "An Invitation to the Criticism of Educational Policies." *The Proceedings of the Philosophy of Education Society*, 1976.

_____, and Jonas F. Soltis. "Locating Teacher Competency: An Action Description of Teaching." *Educational Theory* 24 (1974).

Kleinig, John. "R. S. Peters on Punishment." *British Journal of Educational Studies* 20 (1972): 259–269.

Kliebard, Herbert M., "Structure of the Disciplines as an Educational Slogan." *Teachers College Record* 66 (April 1965).

Komisar, B. Paul. "More on the Concept of Learning." *Educational Theory* 15 (July 1965).

Langford, G. "Education." *Proceedings of the Philosophy of Education Society of Great Britain* 2 (January 1968): 31–41.

Macmillan, C. J. B. "Questions and the Concepts of Motivation." *The Proceedings of the Philosophy of Education Society*, 1968.

Marshall, J. D. "Punishment and Education." *Educational Theory* 25 (Spring 1975).

_____. "The Concept of Teaching." *Proceedings of the Philosophy of Education Society of Great Britain* 9 (July 1975): 105–118.

Martin, Jane Roland. "Basic Actions and Education." *Educational Theory* 24 (Winter 1974).

_____. "Can There Be Universally Applicable Criteria of Good Teaching?" *Harvard Educational Review* 33 (Fall 1963).

_____. "On 'Knowing How' and 'Knowing That.' " *The Philosophical Review* 67 (1959).

Martin, Michael. "Gribble on Roland's Analysis of Knowledge." *Educational Theory* 11 (1971).

Mays, Wolfe. "Linguistic Analysis and the Philosophy of Education." *Educational Theory* 20 (1970).

McClellan, James E. "In Reply to Professor Soltis." *The Proceedings of the Philosophy of Education Society*, 1971.

McNeill, John L. "Justified True Belief." *The Proceedings of the Philosophy of Education Society*, 1976.

_____. "Recognizing Teaching and Some Related Acts." *The Proceedings of the Philosophy of Education Society*, 1975.

Morgan, Kathryn. "Rationality, Madness and Pedagogical Witchcraft: The Dangers of 'Mental Health' as an Aim of Education." *The Proceedings of the Philosophy of Education Society*, 1974.

Morshead, Richard W. "Some Inadequacies in Hardie's Conception of Educational Concepts." *Studies in Philosophy and Education* 2, no. 4 (Winter 1963).

Murphy, F. "The Paradox of Freedom in R. S. Peters' Analysis of Education as Initiation." *British Journal of Educational Studies* 21 (1973): 5–33.

Noddings, Nel. "A Pedagogical View of 'Knowing That' and Knowing How.' " *The Proceedings of the Philosophy of Education Society*, 1975.

_____. " 'Reasonableness' as a Requirement of Teaching." *The Proceedings of the Philosophy of Education Society*, 1976.

_____. "Teacher Competency: An Extension of the Kerr-Soltis Model." *Educational Theory* 24 (1974).

Nyberg, David. "Skill School v. Education School: An Essay on Carl Bereiter's Pedagogics." *Educational Theory* 26 (Spring 1976).

Oakeshott, Michael. "Political Education." In *Philosophy and Education*, ed. by I. Scheffler. 2d ed. Boston: Allyn and Bacon, 1966.

O'Connor, D. J. "The Nature of Educational Theory." *Proceedings of the Philosophy of Education Society of Great Britain* 6 (January 1972): 97–109.

Olford, John E. "The Concept of Creativity." *Proceedings of the Philosophy of Education Society of Great Britain* 5 (January 1971): 77–95.

Oliver, R. G. "Knowing the Feelings of Others: A Requirement for Moral Education." *Educational Theory* 25 (Spring 1975).

Page, Ralph C. "Opportunity and Its Willing Requirements." *The Proceedings of the Philosphy of Education Society*, 1976.

Pap, Arthur. "The Role of Analytic Philosophy in College Education." *Harvard Educational Review* 26 (Spring 1956).

Parsons, Michael. "Review Essay—J. F. Soltis' *An Introduction to the Analysis of Educational Concepts.*" *Educational Theory* 19 (1969).

Peters, R. S. "Education and the Educated Man." *Proceedings of the Philosophy of Education Society of Great Britain* 4 (January 1970): 5–20.

Phillips, Hollibert E. "Rationality and Schooling." *The Proceedings of the Philosophy of Education Society*, 1974.

Popp, Jerome A. "Studying." *The Proceedings of the Philosophy of Education Society*, 1975.

Powell, John P. "Teaching Successfully and Just Teaching." *Educational Theory* 18 (1968).

Pratte, Richard. "Innovation in Education." *The Proceedings of the Philosophy of Education Society*. 1974.

_____. "The Concept of Cultural Pluralism." *The Proceedings of the Philosophy of Education Society*, 1972.

Price, Kingsley. "The Sense of 'Performance' and Its Point." *The Proceedings of the Philosophy of Education Society*, 1974.

_____. "What Is a Philosophy of Education?" *Educational Theory* 6 (April 1956).

Riegle, Rodney P. "Classifying Classroom Questions." *The Proceedings of the Philosophy of Education Society*, 1976.

_____. "The Concept of 'Learning.' " *The Proceedings of the Philosophy of Education Society*, 1973.

Robinson, K. "The Task-Achievement Analysis of Education." *Educational Philosophy and Theory*, October 1972.

_____. "Worth-While Activities and the Curriculum." *British Journal of Educational Studies* 22 (1974): 34–55.

Rozycki, Edward G. "Measurability and Educational Concerns." *Educational Theory* 24 (Winter 1974)

_____. "The Functional Analysis of Behavior." *Educational Theory* 25 (Summer 1975).

Ryle, Gilbert. "Thinking and Self-Teaching." *Proceedings of the Philosophy of Education Society of Great Britain* 5 (July 1971): 216–228.

Scheffler, Israel. "Toward an Analytic Philosophy of Education." *Harvard Educational Review* 24 (Fall 1954).

Schrag, Francis. "Teaching/Healing: The Medical Analogy." *Record* 72 (1971): 594–604.

Scriven, Michael. "Truisms as the Grounds for Historical Explanations." In *Theories of History,* ed. by Patrick Gardiner. New York: The Free Press, 1959.

Serafini, Anthony. "Achievements, Illocutions and the Concept of Teaching." *Educational Theory* 26 (Spring 1976).

Shermis, Sherwin S. "On Becoming an Intellectual Discipline." *Phi Delta Kappan* 44 (November 1962).

Silk, David Neil. "Aspects of the Concept of Authority." *Educational Theory* 26 (Summer 1976).

Smith, B. Othanel. "A Concept of Teaching." *Teachers College Record* 61 (February 1960).

Snook, Ivan A. "Indoctrination and the Indoctrinated Society." *Studies in Philosophy and Education* 8 (1973).

_____. "Neutrality and the Schools." *Educational Theory* 22 (1972).

_____. "Teaching Pupils to Think." *Studies in Philosophy and Education* 8 (1973).

_____. "The Concept of Indoctrination." *Studies in Philosophy and Education* 7 (1970).

Soltis, Jonas F. "Analysis and Anomalies in Philosophy of Education." *The Proceedings of the Philosophy of Education Society,* 1971. Also in *Educational Philosophy and Theory,* 1971.

_____. "Men, Machines and Morality." In *The Proceedings of the Philosophy of Education Society,* 1966. Also in *Value Theory and Problems in Education,* ed. by P. Smith. Urbana: University of Illinois Press, 1971.

_____. "Learning Patterns." *Focus on Learning* 1 (1971).

_____, with Donna Kerr. "Locating Teacher Competency: An Action Description of Teaching." *Educational Theory* 24, no. 1 (Winter 1974). Also in *Pedagogische Studien* 52, no. 3 (March 1975).

_____. "On Defining Education: An Apology." *The Proceedings of the Philosophy of Education Society,* 1969.

_____. "Philosophy of Education: A Fourth Dimension." *Teachers College Record* 67 (April 1966).

_____. "Philosophy of Education: Retrospect and Prospect." In *The Proceedings of the Philosophy of Education Society* 1975. Also in *Educational Theory* 25, no. 4 (Fall 1975).

_____. "The Concept of Assessment: A Response to Mr. Flew." *The Proceedings of the Philosophy of Education Society,* 1973.

_____. "The Language of Visual Perception." In *Psychological Concepts in Education,* ed. by Komisar and McMillan. Chicago: Rand McNally, 1967. Also in *Human Development and Cognitive Processes,* ed. by J. Elliot. New York: Holt, Rinehart & Winston, 1971.

_____. "The Passion to Teach." *Theory into Practice,* February 1973.

_____. "The Subjective Dimension of Explanation." *The Proceedings of the Philosophy of Education Society,* 1965.

Stevenson, C. L. "The Scientist's Role and the Aims of Education." *Harvard Educational Review* 24 (Fall 1954).

Strain, John Paul. "A Critique of Philosophical Analysis in Education." *Educational Theory* 14 (July 1964).

Strike, Kenneth A. "Freedom, Autonomy and Teaching." *Educational Theory* 22 (1972).

_____. "T. F. Green on Knowledge and Belief." *The Proceedings of the Philosophy of Education Society,* 1972.

_____. "The Logic of Neutrality Discussions: Can a University Be Neutral?" *Studies in Philosophy and Education* 8 (1973).

_____. "Thinking on Thinking: Some Logical and Ethical Considerations." *The Proceedings of the Philosophy of Education Society,* 1971.

Swift, Leonard F. "Explanation." In *Language and Concepts in Education,* ed. by B. O. Smith and R. H. Ennis. Chicago: Rand McNally, 1961.

Terris, Martin. "The Distinction between 'Knowing How' and 'Knowing That' Defended and Its Relevance to Education Defined." *The Proceedings of the Philosophy of Education Society,* 1970.

Tostberg, Robert E. "Observations on the Logical Basis of Educational Policy." *Educational Theory* 25 (Winter 1975).

Waks, Leonard J. "Education and Meta-Ethics." *Studies in Philosophy and Education* 6 (1969).

_____. "Knowledge and Understanding as Educational Aims." *Monist* 52 (1968).

_____. "Mr. Antony Flew on Teaching and Testing." *The Proceedings of the Philosophy of Education Society,* 1973.

_____. "Re-examining the Validity of Arguments Against Behavioral Goals." *Educational Theory* 23 (1973).

Wall, G. I. "The Concept of Vocational Education." *Proceedings of the Philosophy of Education Society of Great Britain* 2 (January 1968): 51–65.

Watt, A. J. "Conceptual Analysis and Educational Values." *Educational Philosophy and Theory,* October 1973.

_____. "Forms of Knowledge and Norms of Rationality." *Educational Philosophy and Theory,* March 1974.

White, Alan R. "Needs and Wants." *Proceedings of the Philosophy of Education Society of Great Britain* 8 (July 1974): 159–180.

White, Thomas I. "The University Community and Political Ends: A Critical Examination." *The Proceedings of the Philosophy of Education Society,* 1974.

Wilbanks, Jan J. "Educational Reductionism." *Educational Theory* 24 (Winter 1974).

Wilson, John B. "Comment on Flew's 'What Is Indoctrination?' " *Studies in Philosophy and Education* 4, no. 4 (Summer 1966).

_____. "The Justification of Punishment." *British Journal of Educational Studies* 19 (1971): 211–212.

Withey, Donald A. "Education, Initiation, and Innovation." *Educational Theory* 25 (Spring 1975).

Index